LOSS OF FAITH

Patricia Milner

©2014
Nightengale Press
A Nightengale Media LLC Company

LOSS OF FAITH

Copyright ©2014 by Patricia Milner
Cover Design ©2014 by Nightengale Press

All rights reserved. Printed in the United States of America. No part of this book may be reproduced or transmitted in any form or by any means, electronic or mechanical, including photocopying, recording, or by any information storage and retrieval system without written permission from the publisher, except for the inclusion of brief quotations in articles and reviews.

If you purchased this book without a cover, you should be aware that this book is stolen property. It was reported as "unsold and destroyed" to the publisher, and neither the author nor the publisher has received any payment for this "stripped book."

For information about Nightengale Press please
visit our website at www.nightengalepublishing.com.
Email: publisher@nightengalepress.com

Library of Congress Cataloging-in-Publication Data

Milner, Patricia,
LOSS OF FAITH/ Patricia Milner
ISBN 13: 978-1-935993-59-9
Memoir

Copyright Registered: 2014
First Published by Nightengale Press in the USA

March 2014

10 9 8 7 6 5 4 3 2 1

Printed in the USA and the UK

Dedication and Acknowledgements

I have written this book to help people heal: to know its all right to be different from others and to have visions and experiences that many people never have in their entire lifetime. It is a privilege and honour to have insight and compassion for those who are not as fortunate as we are. My dream was to be able to show people no matter what you go through or what life throws as you there is a future where we can bring in positive changes and life really is worth living. The freedom of the new filled with love and excitement in a new way of being.

I want to dedicate this book to my father, Robert Milner, who was a very special influence in my life. He was an exceptional person who gave me strength and courage. I also want to dedicate this book to my daughter who I love so much and will remain special in my life, always.

In addition, I would like to my editor Linda Woods and my publisher Valerie Connelly who have helped me become the writer I am. They are an inspiration to me.

Chapter One

Going Home

As I walked into the kitchen, Mother was following and needling me, "What's going on and why all this stuff?"

"Mother, for once in your life, give me a break," I said, as I pushed past her to get to the living room and my dad.

"Ada, leave the girl alone and just let her sit down," Father said in frustration.

"I have left Trevor," I blurted out.

"You can't do that. You are married and have a child to consider," Mother said, her voice rumbling like thunder across stormy gray skies as she placed her hands on her hips in disgust. "I am thinking of my child, that's why I am here but if you don't want me I will go find somewhere else to stay," I cried, and stood up to leave.

"Sit down, Patricia, you are not going anywhere. Mother, go and make the girl a cup of tea," Father insisted.

Besides my father working full time, he was also a medium and spiritual healer and was very perceptive.

LOSS OF FAITH

"I knew you were coming home," he said. "I have felt your pain for a long time, but last night, I saw you with suitcases entering this house. So, I will sort this out with your mother. Don't worry." My father was so gentle with his words.

"I just could not take it anymore," I said. "His debts, people he owed money to, wanting to clear those debts by having sex with me, on his say so. When I would not do it, he got funny with me, stayed out at night, and did not talk to me. He would not allow my friends to come to the house and that kept me isolated. I felt so alone. His whole family has been on my case, pressuring me by trying to take over control of my daughter. The rows we have been having are affecting both Angela and me. I have not said anything to you because I thought I could cope and sort it out myself. I blocked you, so you could not pick it up," I cried.

"I know, Patricia, but I could still feel your pain, so I knew there was something wrong," he said as his voice filled with sadness , like the cry of a wolf in the forest at night.

"You should have trusted that you could talk to me," he said.

"I know, Father, but I just did not want to worry you until I had sorted out what I was going to do," I replied.

"If you think you are bringing shame to this family by getting divorced, you have another thing coming," Mother screamed in a high pitched voice that pierced my eardrums as she stormed like a regimental soldier into the living room and thrust a cup of tea at me. "You can just go back to him and make the best of it," she said, growling

LOSS OF FAITH

like an old bull frog

"So, I can't even have a private conversation with my father. You have to earwig and interfere, as always. Why did you have me, Mother? Why? You can't stand me. I can never do anything right. Every time I breathe, I feel that you wished it was my last breath. So, just go away and leave me to talk with my father," I screamed, bursting into tears.

"I have just about had enough of an unloving, uncaring mother. I hate you," I shouted, my voice quivering and my body shaking all over."

"Did you hear that, Bob? I have never been so insulted in all my life. Are you going to let her talk to me like that?" she asked angrily while stomping around the living room and banging things about.

"Ada, just go and do something in the kitchen with Angela and leave us alone to talk. She did not mean it. She is just upset," he replied.

"Taking her side again," she said.

"Ada, please go and do something else now," he said, raising his voice and giving her that look that said *enough*. My father's eyes said it all, a stern and no nonsense look that always shut my mother up.

Mother hurried to the kitchen, muttering under her breath.

I burst into tears. I could hardly get my breath, my heart pounding and my pulse racing. My tears running down my face like Niagara falls. It seemed never ending. It was difficult to get my words out as I sobbed my heart out. I talked to my father about everything that had happened during my marriage with Trevor. I just could not stop until everything came out and I was exhausted from all the emotions.

He listened intently and watched until I stopped.

"Have you had something to eat?" he asked.

"No, not for a while" I replied.

"What do you want?" he enquired.

"Not much, just a sandwich," I said, wiping the tears from my eyes.

"Ada, make the girl a sandwich. She's hungry," he said.

Father and I both sat in silence looking at the orange flames bouncing erratically in the open fire until Mother hurried in and just about threw the sandwich at me.

"Here you are," she said angrily. She hated me. I could feel the tingly icicles in my body just by her presence.

Angela followed and sat by my side silently on the sofa, clinging to me like glue, sucking her thumb.

"Can you make us both a cup of tea, Mother?" Father asked.

She hurried off in silence and came back with two cups of tea.

"Thanks Mother. Now sit down and we will talk," he said.

"She is going right back to her husband and make the most of it. She is not bringing shame to this family. No one has ever gotten a divorce—ever. Whether they have been happy or unhappy, they have stayed with their husbands," she hurriedly said as she sat down with a thump.

"Oh, so that's it. It is not about me or Angela, it's about

you. What shame? Why should I stay unhappy? Do you know you make me sick because all you can think about is what the neighbours will say? You are pathetic, Mother. You value the neighbours' opinion over your daughter's happiness. You are so shallow. I just can't believe what I am listening to," I shouted as I got up and walked quickly away with Angela running after me, crying.

"See what you have done?" I said to my mother, bending down to pick up Angela, holding her tight as I talked to her to calm her down.

"You just can't leave anything alone can you? I am not going to bring Angela up with rejection like you've given me."

"Mother, that's enough. She is not going back. We just have to sort things out here for her to stay and I don't want to hear any more about it. So, make up the spare bed so she can sort out Angela and the room she is staying in," Father said with a stern but calm tone.

Mother started opening her mouth to interrupt saying, "So…"

"No, Ada. No more. Just do as I ask and leave things alone. We all need some peace and quiet and sleep. Tomorrow is another day," he said.

Mother hurried off upstairs in a temper, throwing her arms around and stamping her feet like a child.

"Come and sit down, Patricia," Father said.

I walked over to the settee and sat down, placing Angela on my lap.

"It will be all right Patricia, don't worry," Father said as he sat on the settee, placed his arms around me and held me tight. That meant so much to me. Angela sat on

LOSS OF FAITH

my lap snuggled into me sucking her thumb.

"When is daddy coming?" Angela quietly asked as she sat up.

"He's not coming Angela," I replied looking into her puzzled face.

"Why is grandma shouting, does she not like us anymore?" Angela said.

Before I could say anything, father reached over picking up Angela and sitting her on his knee saying, "Of course Grandma likes you both. She is just not happy right now."

"Why is Grandma not happy?" Angela asked.

"Grandma just has a lot to do, that's all," he replied.

"Come on Angela, let's do some drawing," Father said as he placed Angela on the floor and got the colouring books and pencils. I watched them together chattering away to each other. I am sure father was enjoying it more than Angela. I sat quietly with my thoughts.

It was some time before Mother came down stairs, but suddenly you could hear the heavy footsteps coming down the creaking stairs, my heart pounding to every step, dreading the moment she would come back into the living room. Suddenly, the stairs door flung open and Mother said, snapping, "The bed is made up so you can sort things out for yourself now," just like a child throwing its teddy out of the pram.

"All right, I will take things upstairs so I can get Angela ready for bed," I replied.

Chapter Two

Settling In

I struggled to carry Angela and my heavy old black suitcase upstairs. There was not much light on the stairs as there was only one small window to one side at the top of the stairway. The stairway also felt a bit cold and eerie. I never liked being there for long. So I rushed up the stairs, Angela in my arms, dragging my suitcase behind me. I ran into the bedroom, placed Angela on the bed and threw my suitcase on the rickety old bed. The bedroom hadn't changed much from my childhood. It still had the old bed with springs and the picture rails on the walls. The old fashioned, dark wood wardrobe and matching chest of drawers. Cream flowery curtains to match the brown carpet and a white patterned net curtain across the window so no-one could see in. The old metal frame window looking out at the houses across the street. It was like walking down memory lane. Stuck in that moment of time, I unpacked my suitcase, got things out for bedtime and walked across the landing to the bathroom. The frosted window overlooking the back garden and the asbestos garage which was dad's pride and joy. The white metal bath with its shaped legs and old fashioned taps standing on the floor in front of the window, the old sink and toilet with a wooden cover by its side. I ran the bath water while undressing Angela.

"Are we staying with Grandma?" Angela asked. My heart sank like a lead balloon.

"Yes, for now," I replied my heart, pounding in panic.

"Is Daddy coming?" she asked, looking straight into my eyes.

"No, sweetheart, he is staying at home," I said, my voice beginning to quiver. I quickly pulled her towards me, holding her tight so she could not see the tears rolling down my cheeks.

Taking a deep breath to pull myself together, I said, "Come on, let's get you washed." I picked her up and placed her in the bath. She loved the water, so I knew it would take her mind off things. She started splashing and giggling and we had a water fight as I washed her. I was trying to keep everything as normal as I could for her, but it was not easy. My mind was in so much pain from the stress, I felt my head was being crushed in a vice and my heart was shattering into a million pieces. I pulled her from the bath water and placed her in a bath towel. Then, I pulled the bath plug out. She was giggling and wriggling as I tickled her tummy. She had such an infectious laugh, I could not help but laugh with her. Getting her dressed was always a fight, but eventually it was done, and I put her into bed.

LOSS OF FAITH

"Where are you sleeping?" she asked.

"With you," I replied. That seemed to make her happy. She looked so tiny in the double bed. "What shall I sing for you tonight?" I asked.

"Ba, Ba, Black Sheep," she giggled. This was her favourite nursery rhyme. I started to sing. "Ba, Ba, black sheep have you any wool? Yes sir, yes sir, three bags full. One for the master and one for the dame, and one for the little boy who lived down the lane."

"Again mummy?" she asked. I kept singing it as she watched me, her eyelids slowly closing while she sucked her thumb. She looked so peaceful, my beautiful little girl. She was all I had in the world and I loved her so much. As I watched her drop to sleep, tears ran down my cheeks. I waited until she was sound asleep and made sure she was tucked in tightly and kissed her forehead.

What am I going to do?

While upstairs, I could hear Mother's voice droning like an irritating noise in the background, one of those whines you desperately want to find and switch off. Going on and on at my father about the shame and how I should go back. But by this time, I could not have cared, even if it meant I had to find somewhere else to stay.

I took a deep breath and walked downstairs. I opened the stair doors into the living room where there was an old-fashioned, yellow, lead fireplace with an open fire that heated the water. An oven stood to the right of the fireplace and a pull down door revealed a hidden shelf above it, where my mother used to keep firewood. It had two silver metal buffets with red seats covers which were joined together by a thin silver metal piece running from one buf-

LOSS OF FAITH

fet to the other. An old-fashioned fire guard stood in front of the open fire. There was a Sixties writing bureau under the window. On the back wall was my father's pride and joy—his piano. There was an Alsatian dog statue in the centre of the piano top and two pink flowery small vases either side. These sat on crochet mats my grandmother had made. The room window looked out across the front garden and across the street at the houses opposite. A white patterned net hung to stop anyone looking in. The curtains were green to match the carpet and three piece suite. A small television sat on a table in the corner of the room. Either side of the fireplace were built in cupboards and drawers painted white which were my father's favourite place for all that he would not throw away. As I walked into the living room Mother instantly stopped talking. There was this deadly silence—one that confirms that you were the topic of conversation just before you entered.

I sat in the silence with my arms folded out of boredom for a while as Mother watched her usual Coronation Street. She sat intensely her eyes glued to the television. No-one was allowed to speak while it was on. I hated *Coronation Street*.

My anxiety about the future (what I was going to do and how I was a going to manage) welled up inside me. My stomach was full of knots and butterflies.

Is this what my life was all about: tragedy after tragedy, never finding true love and happiness? At the moment, it could not get any worse.

I had left Trevor with all of Angela's clothes and toys. I only had three skirts, some jumpers, two pairs of shoes, a coat, my underwear, night clothes and very little money.

LOSS OF FAITH

I knew I would have to speak to my boss at work in the morning. What was I going to do? I knew Mother would do nothing to help me, so, most likely, I would have to pack my job in and look after my daughter.

After *Coronation Street* had finished, Mother turned to me her arms folded and said in a sharp voice, "Ok, you have decided you are not going back to Trevor, but I'm going to make it very clear to you. You have a daughter and I'm not looking after her while you go to work or want to go out anywhere. You will have to bring her up on your own with no help from me. You will pay board and lodging for both of you and you will do everything for you and Angela. I will have nothing to do with it."

"If you think I expected anything from you, Mother, you are wrong. All of my life, you've never given me anything, not even love, so why should I expect that it's going to be any different now? If you think that your being like this will make me go back to Trevor, you are sadly mistaken. It makes me even more determined to make a life for myself and Angela. I just don't know how anyone could end up with a mother like you. You don't care what I've gone through or how I've had the courage to do this to make a better life. You should never have had children, especially me, because all I am to you is a burden. I'm going to bed as it's the only place I will get some peace, from you constantly going on and putting me down. In fact, why don't you just drive a stake through my heart and be done with it? You have no compassion," I said, my voice quivering as I got up angrily and stormed out of the living room door and slamming the door behind me to go upstairs to bed.

LOSS OF FAITH

My heart was in pain as though I had been stabbed through my heart and the tears streamed like a waterfall down my face. I felt sad that no one loved me, feeling all on my own. Even my dad could not keep taking my side as he would get it in the neck from my mother. If it were not for my daughter, I would have ended my life. She was the one person who kept me going. I loved her so much. I could not stop crying as I washed and changed for bed. I slipped quietly into bed and held onto the one true thing in my life – Angela. I held her tightly close to my heart. I loved her with all my heart. At that moment, a white light appeared in the bedroom and my angel, Raphael, came through with his colours of blue and green and a warm smile.

"Don't be sad, Patricia. You have made the right choice and there will be a lot more choices and decisions to come over the next twelve months," he said in his calm loving voice.

"But, why do I have to suffer with so much pain in my heart? Why me? Why can't I just have a happy normal life, like everyone else? Why can't I have a mother who can understand and give me love when I need it? I need it right now, not tomorrow, next week or next year, but now," I cried. I could hardly catch my breath between each word. My heart pounding and racing with the pain I felt inside. Lost, alone, unhappy and unloved.

"Rest now Patricia. You will understand," he replied. The bedroom glowing from his light.

"How can I rest? You only appear when I am unhappy. I have not seen you for some time and now when I'm at my worst, you come to me. Why can't you help me before

LOSS OF FAITH

things happen? Then, I could understand that you are trying to help me. Oh, just go away and leave me alone. You can't love me and allow me to keep getting hurt. This is all stupid and unreal, and I hate you, so go away," I cried as I buried my head under the covers to block him out.

As fast as Raphael appeared, he disappeared, followed by the white light.

It's all rubbish. I do not want my daughter to go through what I have gone through. I want to protect her from all this.

I felt so unhappy. Tears were streaming down my face and I cried myself to sleep, feeling so alone.

I was awakened the next morning by Angela who was playing with my nose and hair. I opened my eyes and she was giggling. I smiled, kissed her, and gave her a big hug. She made me so happy.

"Come on, Angela. It's time to get up, get washed and then, we can have breakfast," I said as I picked her up and got out of bed.

I walked to the bathroom and started running the bath. Bath time was always fun. We both liked water and it was inevitable that water fights always began. I made sure this bath time was no different from before. We played and laughed whilst inside, I felt empty and so full of pain in my heart.

Chapter Three

Boss to the Rescue

After we bathed and dressed, we went downstairs to get breakfast. The kitchen was small with the pantry door to the right next to the back door. The sink was under the window, which over looked the back garden. The old fashioned Ada washing machine with it electric rollers was in the left corner of the kitchen next to the gas cooker. An old arm chair huddled in the corner next to the tiled fireplace that is blocked off, where Father's dog Bess, a black and tan mixed variety was laying down. It was her place to sit and sleep. Father loved his dogs. Everyone of them, as far as I could remember, was called Bess. The kitchen table was pushed against the wall. It was yellow Formica with matching chairs. The table was laid for breakfast. Brown lino covered the wooden floor boards and a brown and beige rug was by the back door to wipe your feet on. Cream curtains hung at the kitchen window. Mother was meticulous over how the house was kept. Nothing out of place. Father had gone to work and Mother was busy washing dishes at the kitchen sink. She never turned to look at me or said a word as I walked into the kitchen to get breakfast for both of us.

She just wiped her hands and walked into the living room out of our way. I couldn't be bothered with her. We had cereals for breakfast as always. After breakfast, I washed up as I remembered Mother's words, "You have to do everything yourself." Silence prevailed and it was uncomfortable.

Angela, being Angela, asked, "Why is Grandma not talking to us?"

"Grandma is not feeling well," I replied.

How could she be like this with my daughter?

"Right, Angela, we must put our coats on to go out," I said, as Mother came back into the kitchen and started wiping down the sink.

Mother sharply turned her head. Her hands still in water, cleaning the sink.

"Where are you going?" Mother demanded in an angry voice.

"I have to go to work to explain what is happening and try and get an appointment with a solicitor," I replied as I walked towards the back door to leave.

"Well, remember, we are not keeping you," she grumbled, giving me a dirty look.

"I've been through all of that. I know you have no intention of helping me so just shut up and leave me alone. Just get off my back. You need to know something too. I don't care what happens, but the one thing I do know is

LOSS OF FAITH

I am not going back to Trevor under any circumstances —even if I have to live on the street. So get that into your head and just get off my case," I snapped.

That created a silence I could never forget. I was older and had my own opinions that she could not influence. I had been married and made my own decisions. The final thing was that I was over twenty-one and there was nothing she could do.

I had left Trevor with no money, no car and no clothes, but within my heart I felt freedom and I had my daughter.

I picked up Angela and stormed out of the kitchen and went upstairs to get her ready.

"Why is Grandma so angry with us? Does she not like us?" Angela asked, tears rolling down her face.

"Grandma is just not feeling well, that's all," I replied pulling her towards me and cuddling her until her tears had stopped.

"Everything will be all right Angela you will see," I said looking at her while I stroked her head and wiped her tears away.

I dressed Angela in a green dress and white socks and shoes and a green coat, to go out. She kept looking at me a bit puzzled, but what could I say without causing her concern. It was difficult as my heart was so overwhelmed with sadness for her. I started to tickle her belly and make her laugh. I just wanted to take her mind off things and make her happy. She was wriggling and giggling away, she had such an infectious laugh. Now we could set off and go to see my boss at work. We walked down the stairs into the living room still laughing. I could sense the atmosphere from my mother, but it did not matter. We just carried on walking out of the back door laughing as though nothing was the matter.

It took us about twenty minutes to get to the office. As we approached the long building, you could see lots of small windows and big double wooden doors at the entrance. I opened one of the doors, and we walked through into reception. It was set to the right hand side with a tall large corner unit in oak wood with the receptionist sitting behind it. A scenic view painting hung behind her on the wall. It made the right impression to visitors.

My boss saw us walking through the door and invited me into his office. It was to the left of the reception. He had a big circular oak desk with a big leather chair and a picture of wild horses running free in the countryside on the wall behind him. Two double wooden filing cabinets were on the wall to the left of him and a frosted window to the right which let the sun sparkle across the room.

His desk was well organized with filing trays and a large brown leather case that wrapped around the pink blotting paper. A writing pad on top of the blotting paper held a brown pen waiting to be used. Everything was colour coordinated, even the carpet. It was unusual for a man, but he was very fussy with his clothes too. He was a very smart, clean shaven man, a little rotund, but always dressed professionally.

He was a hard but genuine man who only ever thought about work. He walked around his desk and sat down. He wore steel rimmed square glasses that sat on the end of his nose. His head dropped as he looked at me with his green eyes over the top of his glasses. I was holding onto Angela, who was leaning on me watching and listening, quietly sucking her thumb. She had never met my boss and his office was a bit intimidating.

"Well Patricia, what happened this morning?" he asked.

"I left my husband last night and have no one to look after my daughter," I replied.

"What about your mother?" he asked.

"She won't do anything. She thinks I should go back and put up and shut up, but I can't. I will be the first divorce in the family and on the street we live on, so it is the shame of it. She will not do anything for me so I am going to have to quit my job," I replied.

"Oh, I am sorry to hear that Patricia. You are good at what you do and you have lots of potential. Are you sure you can't find anyone to look after your daughter?" he enquired.

"No, I can't and I am not going to leave her with just anyone, so my daughter must come first," I said.

"Let me go sort some things out and I will be back in a minute," he said as he left the room.

Angela climbed up onto my knee and was keeping herself amused by playing with the pens and things my boss had placed on his desk. The canteen lady, all dressed in white with a white cap and flat black shoes, walked in and brought me a cup of tea and an orange juice for Angela. We sat and drank our drinks while I waited. Angela was beginning to get restless and it was difficult to keep her sitting without getting into mischief. It really did seem to be forever since my boss had gone. In fact, almost an hour had passed and I was beginning to get fidgety as he walked through the door.

LOSS OF FAITH

"Well, Patricia, I know you can't work because of your circumstances but you are such a good person and worker, that here is what I'm going to do for you. Here is a letter making you redundant. You have a month's salary and a month's redundancy pay plus all your holidays. That should keep you going until you can get yourself sorted out one way or the other. All I want you to do is promise me, when you get things sorted out and find somewhere you can place your daughter that you will come back and talk to me. There will always be a place for you in my business. I think you are very brave to do what you are doing," he said.

I was speechless and overwhelmed with emotions. The tears came streaming down my face. No one had ever been so nice to me before.

"What's up, Patricia? Has the cat got your tongue? It's the first time I've ever seen you lost for words," he said smiling.

"Well, I just did not expect anything. You have always been so hard on me and very tight with money at work," I sobbed.

"Why are you crying, Mummy?" Angela asked.

"I am crying because I am happy, Angela," I replied.

"Ah, so you thought I did not have a heart?" he laughed.

"Well, not quite, but you have taken me by surprise," I replied.

"Well, there is no need to thank me because when you come back to work again, I will make you work twice as hard to pay me back," he laughed. He had such a laugh that it made you smile.

LOSS OF FAITH

"Well, what can I say? Thank you and I will never forget what you have done for me," I said.

He got up and gave me a big hug, saying, "Remember what I have said and don't tell anyone about this. I don't want them to think I've gone soft," he said in a quiet voice as he walked me to the door.

I walked out of the building and onto the street just shell shocked. A little Angel from heaven had just appeared to give me a helping hand — the strangest Angel you could have ever imagined. In all the time I had worked for him, I had never seen this side of him. I had my breathing space to sort myself out and I could get my mother off my back by giving her some money.

Angela and I got the first bus into town, stopped for something to eat in a little cafe and then went to the social security office to hand in the letter and get signed on. I would have money coming in while I decided what to do. The social security office was a depressing old building in need of repair, not the sort of place you really wanted to go. Everything creaked and rattled and the furniture looked like it had been there for donkey's years. All the staff looked miserable and you wondered why they worked there. They certainly did not look like they enjoyed their job. I rushed in and out of the place as it was so depressing and negative. After the social security office, we went to make an appointment with a solicitor who just happened to be free and fit me in to get my divorce started. His office was on the top floor. Unlike my boss's office, his was dark and cold with papers scattered everywhere, but he seemed nice and understanding. Angela was very quiet and clingy, sucking her thumb and looking afraid.

LOSS OF FAITH

It had been a big day for both of us. I cuddled Angela to give her reassurance whilst answering his questions. Before we left, he then made me an appointment to go back to see him in a few days to sign all the paperwork that he had to draw up. He was a nice, tall, thin, well dressed man about forty years old. He told me that we would put in for mental cruelty and that I would get some money and the custody of my daughter. So everything would be fine.

I left the solicitor's office with a spring in my step. I had a productive day and got some money in my pocket.

Time to catch a bus and go home now.

As I was walking from the bus home, I had a vision of Raphael smiling and saying, "I said you had made the right choice and that things would be all right."

But why could you not show me that things would be all right?

"You must learn that help will always come in," he replied, as he disappeared.

As I walked down the driveway, there was Mother standing in the doorway with her arms folded across her chest.

"Where have you been all this time?" she snapped.

"What is it to do with you?" I snapped back as I pushed passed her to find my father was home and having his dinner.

"Oh, is it that time already?" I asked.

"You have been out all this time and your daughter has not been fed," Mother said with anger as she stormed passed me almost knocking me out of the way.

"How do you know what I have done with my daughter? You are wrong because she has been fed as we stopped at a café. So don't poke your nose in where it is not wanted," I snapped, walking into the living room to take our coats off and hang them up.

"You have no money, so don't lie. You can't look after yourself, let alone your daughter," she snapped.

"Father, will you shut her up before I lose it with her? She does not know what she is talking about and I want her off my back, right now," I screamed with anger.

"Mummy why are you shouting?" Angela cried.

I rushed and picked her up, saying, "It's all right Angela. I am okay. Don't worry." My stomach squeezed tight in anger at myself for losing my temper in front of my daughter.

"Ok, you two, let's have less. Sit down at the table, Patricia, and have something to eat with us," Father said.

I got Angela and we both sat at the kitchen table and had something to eat while there was chilling silence in the room.

After we had eaten, I got up and took Angela upstairs for her bath.

"Are we staying at Grandma's?" Angela asked.

"Yes, for now, Angela," I said.

"Everyone is either shouting or not talking," Angela said.

"That's just because we are all trying to sort things out. Don't worry, Angela, it will be all right."

I put her to bed singing her favourite nursery rhymes. She giggled and played with my hair until she fell asleep.

I sat looking at her for awhile as swirls of different colours—Blue, Purple, Yellow, Pink, Green—streamed through the bedroom moving around my head, bringing

LOSS OF FAITH

in a sense of peace. When the colours disappeared, I then went downstairs to the living room and sat near the fire. It was February and the glow of the fire was lovely to watch. I enjoyed sitting next to the fire just staring at the flames in silence.

Mother was sitting on the settee with her legs crossed and arms folded and Father sat relaxed in his chair watching *Coronation Street* on the TV. There was only the sound of the television. Not a word was spoken.

Chapter Four

Father's Predictions

As *Coronation Street* finished Father looked across at me smiling.

"So what's been happening today? Did you have a good day?" he enquired.

"Yes, Father, I did have a good day. I got some money from work, registered with social security for money and went to see a solicitor to file for divorce," I replied with a smile that beamed from ear to ear. I felt relieved and happier inside now. I had some money and knew where I stood with things. Mother could not get at me and that was a relief in its self.

"Well, you certainly sound much happier," he replied, as he glanced at the television.

"Yes, I am. The solicitor explained everything and he said I would be fine," I replied, as I watched the orange flames of the fire dance, twisting and twirling, faces appearing within them, and felt the warmth of the fire on my face.

Mother was keeping quiet. Her eyes fixed on the television, but keeping her ears focused on the conversation between Father and me.

"Well, I see you getting your divorce by September but ending up with nothing," he said, with a calm stillness in his voice as he looked straight into my eyes. An eerie feeling made my whole body shiver and for a few seconds fear and doubt shot into my mind. Mother turned and gave me a look that said *I told you so.*

"Oh, don't be stupid, Father. The solicitor said I would get the custody of Angela and some money, so I will be fine," I replied, shaking my head from side to side and shrugging my shoulders.

"Well, we will see," he replied.

"The solicitor must know what he is talking about Father," I replied. By this time I was beginning to get irritable. I crossed my legs and folded my arms, leaned against the fireplace and looked into the fire.

This is not what I wanted to hear.

The living room went quiet as Coronation Street came back on the television. Nothing could move or breathe while this program was on as Mother watched it constantly and would not miss one episode.

By this time, I was really bored as it was not my sort of thing, so at the commercial break, I got up and said, "I am off to bed so I will see you in the morning."

I picked up Angela and headed upstairs. She always came first, so I bathed her and put her to bed singing her to sleep.

When she had dropped off, I got washed and ready for bed. As I lay there, I looked at the swirling colours running around the room. They made me smile and feel

LOSS OF FAITH

happy. I just could not stop thinking about the day and what had happened. It had been such an amazing day. The one thing that worried me was my father's comment that I would get my divorce by September but end up with nothing. I kept trying to push it out of my mind but it kept coming back.

What if he was right?

"You will have to wait and see Patricia," a voice said.

Oh, not this again—go away.

There was nothing but silence as I lay in bed. I turned over, put my arms around my daughter and pulled her in tight, holding her in my arms while I fell asleep.

I got up the next day remembering a dream. It was about my school days, the people in my year, and in particular, a boy called Steve.

I wonder what all that was about.

We got ready to go down for breakfast.

When we went downstairs into the living room, there was Mother having a cup of tea, sitting in the armchair, with her legs crossed and a stern, serious look on her face.

"Now that you are downstairs, we need to sort out money as I am not keeping you both," she fired at me.

"Don't you like us grandma?" Angela asked, as she leaned into me holding me tight.

Mother did not answer. She just sat staring at us both. I could feel her piercing eyes burning through me.

"Can't I get up and open my eyes before you attack me? I am not exactly going to run away," I snapped as I got hold of Angela's hand and walked off into the kitchen to sort out breakfast.

But no, Mother could not leave it there. She came

stomping with her heavy feet after us into the kitchen.

"Your dad and I have talked, and you can pay £10 a week board for both of you, and I will sort out the food so you owe me £20 for this and next week," she said, holding her hand out.

"You'll get it when I've had my breakfast, so go away before I do something I'll regret," I snapped, sitting down at the table with Angela. She sat quietly like a little angel, looking worried. She did not like raised voices.

"You have an attitude problem," she fired back pointing and wagging her finger at me.

"Oh, Mother, look at yourself first. I just can't be bothered with you. Just go away and let me have my breakfast in peace," I said raising my voice with anger.

Angela burst into tears. "Don't be angry mummy," she cried.

I jumped up and picked her up. "I am not mad with you, I love you," I said, my voice quivering as tears rolled down my face.

I looked at my mother with disgust. "See what you have done now, you have no heart, just a frozen iceberg," I snapped.

She stormed out of the kitchen.

"Come on, Angela, everything will be all right, you'll see," I said, drying her eyes and putting her back on the chair.

"Come on, let's have breakfast then we can do something," I said, sitting in my chair.

Afterwards, I washed the pots, went upstairs, and got the £20.

"You sit on the bed for a minute, Angela. I am just

going to give Grandma something and I'll be back," I said placing her on the bed.

"Okay, Mummy," she relied.

I was so mad! I ran downstairs, flung the living room door wide open and rushed over to my mother who was sitting in the armchair. I was so angry I nearly fell over. I stopped suddenly in front of her, looking at her with hatred. Shaking all over, I threw the money on Mother's lap saying, "There you are—just the right amount—not a penny more or a penny less. Maybe now, you will leave me alone." I turned away rushing off to get Angela from upstairs. I got her and we came downstairs through the lounge. My mother was just sat there looking into the fire. Not a word was spoken as we walked through the lounge into the kitchen and out of the back door.

"What is wrong with Grandma? Does she hate us, Mummy?" Angela said, her big eyes looking up at me.

"No sweetheart, she is just not feeling well," I replied.

If only that were the truth.

But what else could I do or say. Angela could not understand it all and I just wanted her to be happy and feel loved by me.

Everyday, I spent my time wandering around the streets, or visiting friends, as I just could not stay at home with my mother. Life was a bit like being a tramp on the streets, finding somewhere to go to keep out of the way and keep warm and have someone to talk to, as I felt so lost, so alone. The one thing I had that was so precious to me and gave me my reason for living was my daughter. My mother could not take that away from me, ever.

Chapter Five

Dreams Come True

    The weeks were passing slowly, like watching a tortoise walk across an acre of land. When would it ever reach its destination? I just was not one for doing nothing. Everything felt so boring, like watching paint dry. There was no happiness just a face set in concrete, fed up and bored. I had my usual routine during the day and the same recurring dream at night of Steve, a boy from school. He was in a different class than mine and had different friends. So we never had much to do with each other. He was very outgoing and popular with the girls. He would not have known I really existed.

    What is this all about?

    Then, one morning I woke up. The rain was pounding against the window pain and thunder was roaring across the dark skies. I opened the curtains to see fork lightning shoot across the sky lighting up the darkness like turning a light switch on.

    Another boring day. What can I do in this weather? Visit

LOSS OF FAITH

my friend Susan, The thought came into my mind from nowhere.

So I got myself and Angela washed, dressed and we had breakfast in peace as no one was around.

"Where are we going, Mummy?" Angela asked as I put her raincoat on.

"We are going to see Susan and Mike," I replied.

"Mike plays games with me. I like him," she replied.

"I am sure he will play games with you if he is at home," I said, as I put my raincoat on and headed out of the door with Angela's hand in mine. I left just in time as Mother was walking down the path heading in our direction, looking like a drowned rat. She passed us in a hurry, holding her head down and not uttering a word. But that didn't matter as we were going out for a while.

We had a long walk in the rain to get to Susan's, but we made it. They lived in a terraced house which was on the main road. The front door was never used so we walked round to the back. All the backs of the terraced houses were open with the old brick built toilets away from the houses. There were no dividing walls just rows and rows of washing lines all tied from the wall of the houses to the brick toilet blocks. Susan's house was in the middle so we had to duck the washing lines to get to her back door.

As I knocked on the back door and opened it, Angela rushed in shouting, "Susan!"

"Hello babes, let's get your wet coat off," Susan replied.

Susan had two children, a boy and a girl.

"Go and play with Alan and Samantha," Susan said.

Off Angela ran into the living room where Susan's

LOSS OF FAITH

kids were playing. Samantha was Angela's age and Alan was a year older. They always played well together and it gave me chance to relax. I took my wet coat off and hung it over the back of the chair. The kitchen was the centre of the house where everything happened. The window overlooked the back yard and had a net curtain and brown heavy curtains hanging to the window sill. A sink unit with cupboards sat under the window. The cooker and washer were to the right of the sink. There was a fireplace on the central wall with a nice warm glowing open fire going. A two-seater brown sofa was on the wall opposite the window and the kitchen table was in the centre of the room. The floor had brown tiles with a mat to dry your feet by the door. There were some shelves up on the walls with a mix of Sixties ornaments. The house was messy but cosy.

Susan and I were just having a cup of tea and catching up on what was happening about things. It was so good to be able to come and relax and feel at peace with someone who was not judgemental about what I was doing.

Half way through the morning her husband, Mike, walked in with a friend. It was Steve from school.

"You too must know each other," Mike said.

I recognized him, but he did not recognize me.

"This is Patricia Milner," Mike said.

"Oh my God, you've changed," Steve said.

"Yes, she has," Mike said.

Steve just kept staring at me.

"Steve broke up with his wife about a month ago," Susan said.

"Are you going to sit down, Steve, and chat with us?"

LOSS OF FAITH

Susan asked.

"Sure," he said, grabbing the chair next to me.

I looked at Susan to see her get up and drag her husband out of the room.

Steve and I chatted for what seemed like ages. We talked non-stop and were so comfortable with each other, laughing and joking. I had not enjoyed myself so much for such a long time.

Suddenly, he looked at his watch and had to go as he was going to be late for work. He gave me a kiss on my cheek and left.

"Well, you two seemed to get on like a house on fire," Susan said.

"Yes, it appears so," I replied, feeling numb.

"Has he asked you out?" she asked.

"No – he had to rush off to work," I said.

"It's really funny, I have been having the same dream every day for ages, about school and about him," I said.

"Well, now you know why. I am sure he will be in touch," Susan said.

"We will see," I said.

"I must go home now to get dinner with my father," I said, as I got up to leave.

"Angela, come and put your coat on, we are going home," I said, popping my head around the living room door.

"Do we have to?" Angela replied.

"Yes we do, so come and put your coat on," I replied, holding her coat.

As we were getting ready to leave, Mike said, "I will drop you home as it's pouring with rain."

LOSS OF FAITH

"Thanks, that will be good," I replied.

We got ready and got in Mike's car and set off for home.

My stomach was in knots and I felt like I was walking on air. It was another miracle.

My dreams are coming true. What I am dreaming is actually happening.

A sense of excitement was moving through my whole body. All this had stopped when I was with Trevor. Now, it is all coming back. There was a skip in my step.

Mike pulled up outside my parent's house and as we were getting out he said, with a smile on his face and that sense of knowing look as he tapped his nose, "Steve will be in touch, I know it."

"We will see, thanks for the ride," I replied closing the door and heading for the house.

As we walked through the door at home, Mother and Father were just sitting down to dinner.

"You look happy today," Father said.

"Yes, I feel happy" I replied.

"There is a letter from your solicitor," Mother said, putting it down by my plate.

"She can open it, when she has eaten," Father said.

We all ate and then I opened my letter.

"I've got to go see the solicitor tomorrow and sign papers and things," I said getting up and walking into the living room with Angela. My thoughts were focused on what had happened today at Susan's. I had never felt my heart race so fast with excitement. *I wonder if I will hear from him.* I couldn't wait for tomorrow to come.

I sorted Angela out, put her into bed, laid at her side

LOSS OF FAITH

and sang songs to her while she dropped off to sleep. The room went hot and a feeling of great love entered the room with circles of white light. I just knew I was not alone and, for such a long time, I felt happy. As I rested there, I watched the circles of white light swirl around the room and I could hear people giggling and someone saying, "Just you wait and see."

Is my life really going to change?

"You wait—just you wait and see," they replied in unison.

A great sense of fatigue came over me.

Chapter Six

Trevor's Threat

The next thing I remember was waking up the next morning with a picture of Steve in my mind's eye. It gave me a warm and comforting feeling inside, like the glow of an open fire on a winter's night. I was still not sure what it was all about but I felt calm inside.

I got up, got Angela ready, and went off to see the solicitor to sign my divorce papers. He told me that Trevor was contesting the divorce but he was not concerned as we had a good case. He said to leave it all in his hands and not to worry. So I signed the papers and left.

On my way home I felt that someone was following me. I kept looking around but could not see anything. It was a creepy feeling, but I knew there was someone there. A sense of fear welled up inside me. It rose from the pit of my stomach, so much so I wanted to be sick. My heart started racing and pounding with panic. I kept looking back, my face rigid. I could not speak. I was trying not to run as I had Angela with me but I could not help my feet picking up pace ready to run, as I was in panic.

"What's a matter, Mummy?" Angela said, her voice trembling as she looked up at me her eyes full of bewilderment.

"It's okay, baby, Mummy just wants to get home quickly as it's cold and we can get home to a warm fire," I replied trying to hold my voice from trembling.

I know something is going to happen, but I have to hold it together for Angela.

We came to the quiet road we had to walk up, but I could feel something was not quite right. Suddenly, a blue saloon car came flying around the corner at high speed screeching its tyres as it pulled up to dead stop beside me. Three men jumped out, lunging at us and grabbed Angela and me, pulling us into the car. It all happened so fast, I wanted to scream. I felt so frightened, my mouth was open, but nothing would come out. I was wriggling trying to get free, but two of them were holding me and pushing me face down onto the back seat of the car, while the other got into the other side with Angela. Angela was crying "Mummy! Mummy!"

"It's okay Angela, Mummy is here," I quickly replied as I reached for Angela and pulled her into my arms, holding her tight. The men pushed us both face down onto the back seat.

They drove at high speed down what appeared to be a back street as the car was bouncing over rough terrain. I couldn't see but I could feel every bump as the car's suspensions bounced over the ground. My heart was pumping with fright. I was clinging to Angela, who was crying

LOSS OF FAITH

as I was trying to comfort her.

"It will be okay, Angela," I said holding tightly into my stomach.

As the car pulled up, they let us sit up and there was Trevor with his friend.

"It's Daddy, Mummy!" Angela said with excitement in her voice.

"Yes, it's Daddy, Angela," I replied. I did not know whether to be afraid or relieved.

"Get out of the car," Trevor said, his voice full of confidence and control. He was happy to see that I was afraid, as there was an air of superiority in his voice and the way he was standing and acting like the *Terminator*. I got out of the car with Angela, and she ran over to Trevor. I looked at Trevor.

What a sick bastard.

"Daddy, Daddy!" Angela said, as she held her arms open and up for him to pick her up.

"Go back to your Mummy, Angela," he said as he pushed her back towards me.

He looked with piercing eyes straight through me as though I was something that had crawled from under a stone that he could just tread on and kill so easily. It sent shivers down my spine.

I grabbed Angela and picked her up.

"Mummy what's up with Daddy? Why does Daddy not want me?" Angela said crying, tears streaming down her face as she leaned into my shoulder.

"It will be okay, baby," I replied. My face filled with hate for the man I had once loved, or so I thought. My only thought was for my daughter and keeping her safe.

LOSS OF FAITH

"You can stop the divorce now or you will never see Angela again," Trevor said in a threatening demanding voice, looking brave in front of his so-called friends. Then, they all piled into the car and drove off, leaving us both standing there breathing in the dust from the dirt road. I held Angela's and my head down, but we were covered in gray dust.

He is not going to get away with this!

I couldn't move. My body frozen still like an iceberg. But those few minutes seemed like a lifetime. My heart was racing with fear and panic, but I was trying to keep it all together for Angela. I just wanted to get home as quickly as possible. It took what seemed for ever for the dust to lift so I could see where I was and get my bearings. I walked quickly while carrying Angela all the way home hugging her and comforting her, telling her it would be all right.

"Why did Daddy not want me?" she cried.

"He does, Angela, he is just having a bad day, that's all," I replied.

What else can I say? I don't have all the answers. That's all I can ever say about anybody.

I passed the old farm and turned the corner to my parent's house. I rushed down the path of my parent's home, pushing open the back door and almost falling into the kitchen. I do not know where my strength had come from to carry Angela all that way, but I just knew I had to keep her safe. By the time I got home, I was exhausted.

My face was white with fear and we were both covered in gray dust as we stood in the kitchen. I could not speak.

LOSS OF FAITH

"What has happened to you?" Father asked with a worried but puzzled look on his face. I could feel my fathers concern and I knew his mind had flashed back to my rape when I was fourteen years old.

I burst into uncontrollable tears. It was as though Niagara falls was falling from my eyes. My words stumbled from my mouth as I gasped for air. I was so frightened, I couldn't breathe.

"Trevor—dragged—us—into—a car. He threatened me!"

Everything came out in a jumble.

"Mummy, Mummy!" Angela cried. She had never seen me like this and I could feel her fear.

"It's okay, Angela," I said, as I tried to calm myself down.

Father jumped off his kitchen chair and rushed over to us both his arms out-stretched.

"Come here, Angela," Father said.

I handed Angela over to Father. He was trying to calm everything down, as usual.

He went and sat on his usual kitchen chair and took Angela's coat off and placed it on the table. My mind was everywhere but nowhere. I was in the kitchen and could see and hear everything but my mind seemed somewhere else—as though I was the watcher, listening to Angela giggle when Father tickled her. But suddenly that moment broke apart.

"I told you not to do this," Mother snapped, looking at me as though I was nothing, while she crossed her legs and folded her arms, with that *I told you* so expression on her face.

LOSS OF FAITH

I hate you, Mother.

"Can't you think of anyone except yourself?" I screamed at her and burst into tears as I fell on my knees to the floor putting my face in my hands. Tears were streaming down my face like a waterfall. I just could not take any more. I was both mentally and physically exhausted. Mother just did not understand anything about me and what I wanted, to be loved and happy, something I could not get from her.

"Ada, leave her alone, that's enough!" Father shouted as he looked down at me with his kind calming eyes. He was trying to keep Angela amused while I could pull myself together.

"What are you going to do?" Father asked.

"He is not going to win. I am going to call the solicitor right now," I cried, getting up and rushing into the living room for the phone.

I could hear Mother and Father talking in the kitchen. They were quietly having words about me. Mother doing her usual about me going back and not bringing trouble to this house, and Father telling her I can stay to sort myself out, and that I was not going back, so she had better get used to the idea.

I got through to my solicitor. I was still crying as I told him what happened. He was going to prepare some papers and come and get me to sign them in the morning. He also was ringing the police for them to come and take a statement.

Mother could hear my conversation with the solicitor so, as soon as I put the phone down, she started up, "Oh, more police, more problems. What will the neighbours say about all these comings and goings? It's bad enough having you and Angela here and having to explain that away, but now, the police and a solicitor," she said angrily.

"Oh, here we go again—like a broken record—what will the neighbours think! What about me?" I screamed as grabbed Angela from my dad and ran off to my bedroom. I held her so tight. I did not want to lose her. I loved her so much.

"Mummy why are you crying?" Angela said, stroking my hair with her hand.

"Mummy's just having a bad day that's all," I replied as I looked at her. I had to smile as she was more the adult, stroking my hair and looking straight into my eyes giving me a look of reassurance. We were both lost in that moment of time. I could still hear Mother and Father talking about me, but I did not care anymore.

Suddenly, I heard footsteps coming up the stairs and Father popped his head around the door, "Are you all right, Patricia?" he asked with a gentle voice.

"Yes, Father. Why does she hate me so much? Can't she see that I have just had a bad experience and all I want is some love for a change?" I cried.

"Your mother has difficulty dealing with things, that's all. Anyway, come downstairs and have some dinner with us," he said, holding his hands out to take Angela.

"Grand-dad can we draw?" Angela asked.

"After dinner, Angela" he said as he picked her up and held her in his arms.

My tears had subsided but I felt sad and afraid inside. *What does the future hold for us?*

We walked down the stairs, through the lounge and

into the kitchen where Mother was silently putting out the dinner. We sat down and not a word was spoken, while we were eating. It was obvious that Mother and Father had had words, but I already knew that from the conversations I could hear from the living room and the rumblings I heard in my bedroom when I was with Angela.

I could always hear everything, whether I was at the bottom of the garden or upstairs. I did not have to be in the same room. Now, that I was away from Trevor, these gifts were coming back and getting stronger as though my mind was now in a better place.

Mother got up, started clearing the table and washing the dishes. So, I picked up Angela and went into the living room to watch television. About an hour later there was a knock at the door and Mother answered it. It was two policemen.

"We have come to see your daughter, Patricia," one said.

"Come into the kitchen and I'll get her," Mother said.

I got up and walked into the kitchen while Father looked after Angela. I could feel Mother's emotions of what will the neighbours think, but there was nothing I could do about it and I tried to push it away.

My father asked them to take a seat.

We all sat at the kitchen table and my father stayed. Mother went into the lounge out of the way.

"We need to take a statement from you, Patricia, regarding the event that happened today," one said. He was tall and skinny, mid-forties, with dark brown hair and green eyes. He asked all the questions. The other officer was in his fifties, stocky, with grey hair and wrote down what we said.

I could remember every detail: the colour and make

of the car, the registration number, the black widow spider tattoo on the neck of one of the men, the serpent tattoo on the arm of the other, the birth mark on the shoulder of the third man, the colour of their eyes and hair, how tall they were, the swinging dice in the car window, the nodding dog on the back window ledge, to the scorpion ring on the forth man's index finger.

Father sat in amazement at the detail I was giving. He looked so proud of me as he knew it wasn't easy for me. I could also feel my father's sadness.

"Your daughter has an amazingly accurate memory," the grey-haired policeman said.

"Yes, she has always been like this and I can promise you that you will find everything spot on," Father replied with pride in his voice.

"Well, this will help us find the people and deal with them," the policeman replied.

"We just need you to sign these papers and we will be on our way, Patricia," the policeman said.

I quickly signed the papers and the policemen left.

The day had been very eventful and I was tired so I picked up Angela, got her ready for bed and laid down with her while she fell asleep.

I was exhausted from the day's events and just lay on the bed peacefully. The bedroom was always cold, but I could feel it heating up as though someone had turned on the oven. The bedroom became hot. A white, wispy light started streaming in and dancing around the room. It felt as though I were floating on clouds, safe and secure, not alone.

The bedroom filled with energy as though there were

LOSS OF FAITH

a hundred people around me, holding me up. The overwhelming feeling of love that came into the room made me cry with joy.

I was not getting the normal dimensional shifts and visions, but my thoughts, feelings, smells, awareness and dreaming were getting stronger. All of my major senses were becoming heightened. I remember feeling this warm glow all around me as though I were being protected. I fell asleep, enveloped in the safety of that warmth.

Chapter Seven

The Solicitor & Steve

When I woke up the next morning, all I could remember was this picture of Steve at my friend's house.

Strange.

I got both of us ready and went downstairs to have breakfast. Mother was cleaning up as she knew the solicitor was coming and everything had to look just so. She was rushing me around to get breakfast over and done with and the pots washed up and put away. It was like being in a hurricane, watching Mother at high speed. No sooner had we finished our cornflakes, our bowls and spoons were snatched from the table, washed, dried and put away. I could smell the disinfectant she had been using, which was not conducive with eating breakfast. She had even put a clean apron on over a clean checked skirt and white blouse. On her feet she had black shoes instead of slippers. She was out to make an impression. Angela was watching Mother zoom around the kitchen. She found it funny and started to giggle. Well it was a bit like a comedy sketch.

"Come on Patricia, get yourself sorted out for the solicitor," Mother snapped as she grabbed our cups from the table and started to wipe it with a wet cloth.

"I am ready. He is only bringing papers for me to sign, that's all," I replied, feeling irritated.

She was out to make an impression and show she was interested and cared, but for me it was too late and false, as she would return to normal after the solicitor had gone, after that show.

Mother was dressed to impress the solicitor. I was in jeans and a T-Shirt.

"Are you not going to get changed?" Mother asked with sarcasm in her voice, looking at me as though I was nothing.

"No, I am what I am," I replied, giving her a filthy look.

There was a knock at the door and Mother rushed to answer it. She knew the solicitor's name as she had heard Father and me talking.

It was the solicitor as I heard Mother say, "Hello Mr. Larkin, please come in."

"Hello, you must be Patricia's Mother," Mr. Larkin replied.

"Yes, I am. Please come this way," mother replied as she showed him into the living room where he sat down in the armchair Mother pointed to.

"Would you like a cup of tea, Mr. Larkin?" Mother asked.

"No, thank you. I won't be here long," he replied.

Mother sat down in her usual armchair with a sense

of importance and Angela and I sat on the settee.

"Hello, Patricia. We had better get started," he said, looking over to me.

He was a balding man in his fifties and looked ancient with a crinkly face and glasses that sat on the end of his nose. He wore a navy blue suit and white shirt with a navy coloured tie, with black shiny shoes that were highly polished. He really was old school.

"Hello, Mr. Larkin. Yes, I would just like to get this over and done with," I replied. My heart started pounding with anticipation as I was nervous and really did not want to relive the traumatic events.

Mother sat listening in as though she was interested and that just annoyed me. Angela snuggled into me sucking her thumb. I gave Mother a look that said I did not want her here, but she stayed anyway just to annoy me.

"Right, Patricia. I want to know what happened yesterday with your husband," he asked looking straight at me over the top of his glasses.

Tears filled my eyes as it had been such an horrific experience I did not want to remember.

"It's all right Patricia, in your own time," he said in a very understanding and calm voice.

We talked about the events the day before, and the police visit. He pulled some papers out of his brief case and turned the pages.

He looked up at me and handed me the papers saying, "I want you to sign these papers. They are for a restraining order to keep Trevor away from you and Angela until we can get him to court."

"Thank you very much," I replied as I signed the papers and handed them back to him.

He packed everything into his brief case and stood up to go. As he got up he looked at me saying, "Everything will be sorted out. You will be all right, Patricia."

"Thank you. I really needed to hear that," I replied.

Mother got up and showed him out and I heard them say their goodbyes and the back door slam shut.

He gave me peace and I felt really calm and relaxed as though a weight had been lifted off my shoulders.

It was about a week later I was sitting in the lounge playing with Angela when the house phone rang. I got up and answered it.

"Hello? It's Mr. Larkin, here," he said.

"Oh! Hello, Mr Larkin," I replied

"The restraining order is now in place and has been served on your husband. The police were very impressed with the accurate detail you have given. When they picked up the men, everything you had described was so perfect that it left nothing to question. The men have been cautioned not to come anywhere near you or they would be prosecuted," he said. That was such a relief to me, my head was somewhere in the clouds. I could not answer.

"Are you there, Patricia?" he asked.

"Yes, Mr Larkin. I heard you and it's such a relief to me, thank you so much," I replied my voice wobbling as tears of relief welled up in my eyes.

"I will talk to you soon when I have more news," he said. I felt he was smiling and happy for me and genuinely was concerned about my well-being.

"Thank you again," I replied as I placed the phone down.

LOSS OF FAITH

My gifts are coming back and getting stronger day by day.

After the solicitor had left, I decided to go and visit my friend Susan as I knew she was off work today. I got Angela ready and we set off walking. It was a lovely sunny day and I felt good. When we got there, Susan wanted to know everything that had happened. Then, she started telling me about a new Crèche that was opening at the Catholic school in the next village.

"But, I am not Catholic," I said.

"You don't have to be, just go and put Angela's name down and see what happens. I'll take you. I've got the car," she said.

"Ok, let's give it a whirl" I replied.

We all got into the car and set off for the school.

It was a very old building with long tall windows with pictures set within the glass. We walked in and spoke to one of the nuns and Angela got a place at the Crèche starting Monday. It was 8:30 a.m. to 4:30 p.m., Monday to Friday, but that did not matter.

Maybe, I could now get a job at my old company.

That did bring a smile to my face as I liked working. I felt things were moving for me again and I knew things would get better.

Angela was playing with the other children while we were talking and she looked happy and was enjoying herself. It always worried me that she did not have any other children to play with or at least very often. But now that was all sorted out.

We left the school. "Susan could we stop at my old company so I can talk to my boss?" I asked.

"Sure," she said, turning the car in the direction of

LOSS OF FAITH

my old workplace. "That's a good idea." Angela stayed in the car with Susan while I went into the building.

My old boss was so pleased to see me and I explained what hours I could work with my daughter in play school. "Come in on Monday and we will have something sorted out for you," he said. "Oh, thank you. I can't wait," I replied.

I could have given him a big hug but he was not that sort of person, so I left feeling a lightness and a spring in my step. I was so happy.

We drove back to Susan's home and when we walked through the door, there was her husband with Steve.

He looked at me and me at him. He could not take his eyes off me. It was embarrassing.

"Well, I think we will leave you two together," Mike said as they both left the room taking Angela along.

"Come on Angela, let's go and do some drawing," Susan said.

"Yes, please," Angela replied excitedly.

Steve and I sat down and talked for hours. I couldn't even tell you what we talked about. We seemed to be in our own little world where nothing seemed to matter.

Then suddenly he said, "Would you like to go out with me sometime?"

"I would love to, but I would have to do it during the day time or on the weekend, as my mother won't baby sit for me," I replied.

My heart had butterflies, feeling excited.

"That's okay. We can do something this weekend. How would you like for us all to go for a picnic in the park?" he asked.

LOSS OF FAITH

He was so calm about it.

"That would be nice," I replied. My heart was beating like a thousand drums. He was cute and not at all what I remembered him to be. At school he was popular with the girls, talkative and full of himself. He did not appear to be like that now.

We arranged a time that he would pick us both up from my mother's the following Saturday. Then, he left.

Angela, Susan, and her husband Mike, came rushing back into the kitchen, and Susan quickly sat beside me excitedly asking, "Well, what happened?" as she placed her hand on my wrist.

"We are going out on Saturday," I replied a bit dazed from it all. I couldn't quite get my words out.

"That's good. He has been asking about you all the time," Mike said with a smile.

I blushed. Everyone noticed and started smiling. Angela climbed on my lap.

"Look at my pictures, Mummy," Angela said.

I took the pictures and looked at the six she had done.

"They are beautiful" I replied. It gave me a chance to get past my blushing and embarrassment.

What a day!

"I better get home or I will be in trouble with my mother yet again," I said, as I got everything together and left.

Things looked so much brighter as we walked home. It was as though I was looking at the world with different eyes. The colours were much brighter and everyone seemed to be smiling and happy, saying "Hello." I felt like I was walking on air, sixteen again, and everyone could

LOSS OF FAITH

see a different me.

When I got home, Mother and Father were in the kitchen. Father looked at me and said, "Well, you look happy today."

"Yes, I am. Everything is good today," I replied, a smile beaming from ear to ear.

I explained what had happened as I was so excited.

"Well, don't look at me for baby sitting while you work or while you're with this Steve fellow. You should not be going out with anyone as you are not even divorced. Everyone will think you left your husband for another man. You should be staying at home and looking after your child and not working," Mother snapped, as she sat back in her chair and folded her arms. My good mood suddenly dropped to the floor like a lead balloon.

"Have you got nothing good to say? Can't I have some happiness without you pulling everything down? It's the Seventies, not 1926. You can't do anything but criticize and pull me down. Well, I tell you something everybody else sees in me what you don't and I will prove something to you one day. Until then, go to hell, Mother," I said angrily as tears rolled down my face.

"Mummy, why are you crying?" Angela asked as she came and held my hand. She was like a little old lady giving reassurance.

"Mummy is all right, Angela, don't worry," I replied as I looked at her and stroked her head.

"Okay, Ada, leave her alone. She has got to do what she wants to do and try and make the best of things for herself," Father said giving her that certain look only he could give that said, "Be quiet."

LOSS OF FAITH

"Oh, taking her side again," Mother snapped, as she crossed her legs defensively

"No, Ada, but let the girl have a life. It's her life, and she is not meant to be on her own. Let her have some fun for a change. Life is too short to be unhappy. So that is enough," Father replied, as he looked at me and smiled.

Mother stood up, pushed her chair back and stomped off like a storm trooper into the living room. Father looked at me and smiled saying, "Never mind your mother. Go for it and I hope you get what you want."

"Thanks Father, that means so much to me," I replied, looking at him and giving a forced smile.

Angela sat quietly. She could always sense when I was upset.

I knew that I was not going to get any help from my mother. I also knew it was not going to be easy working and taking Angela back and forth to the play group. There was going to be a lot of early mornings and a lot of walking to get Angela there and then get to work. But I was determined to do it.

I was all excited because tomorrow, I was going to go out with Steve and Angela for the day. I like Steve. He made me laugh and we liked the same things. I took a walk to the shops with Angela and bought some things to make a picnic basket for the next day.

The excitement made me nervous and I had butterflies in my stomach. I went to bed early with Angela just so I could wake up and it would be Saturday. I was looking forward to getting ready to go out. I did not want my mother to spoil my mood anymore that evening. I just wanted to fall to sleep with that feeling of excitement.

Chapter Eight

My New Romance

Saturday came and I got up early to make sure that we were both ready and the food was all sorted out.

Angela was all excited about going out.

Mother and Father were sitting at the table in the kitchen having breakfast. You could cut the atmosphere with a knife. Father was reading his newspaper, trying to keep out of things. Mother was furious that I was going out with someone else because she still felt I should go back to my husband. She had made that very clear last night. There was only the sound of silence.

Why do I have to go through all this? Why can't Mother just be happy?

"Where are we going, Mummy?" Angela asked, excitedly pulling at my trousers.

"We are going for a picnic in the park," I replied.

"Who's going?" she asked.

"Just you, me, and Steve," I replied as I looked down at her.

LOSS OF FAITH

"Mummy, Mummy," she said.

"Angela, just be quiet for a bit, Baby, and let me get things ready," I replied, feeling harassed and excited at the same time.

"Come on, Angela, come and talk to Granddad," Father said holding out his hands.

As I turned around I caught the eyes of my mother who was not happy about my going. She was sitting with her arms folded and gave me a filthy look.

I just could not be bothered with her. She was not going to spoil my day out under any circumstance. So I turned away and carried on getting things ready.

I had just got packed when Steve's car pulled up outside. I got everything together, looked at my mother and father and said, "I am off now."

"Come on, Angela," I said, holding my hand out.

She came running and grabbed my hand, full of excitement.

"Enjoy yourself," Father replied. As I looked at Mother, she gave me a look of disapproval. It did not matter as I was going out with Steve and Angela to enjoy myself.

Angela was skipping with excitement as we left the house and walked towards Steve's car. As we approached the car, she went all quiet and shy sucking her thumb. That was always a sign of her either being tired or shy.

"Hello. Angela," he said pulling a sherbet lollypop out of his pocket and handing her a brown teddy bear.

She quickly took her thumb out of her mouth.

"What do you say, Angela?" I said, looking at her.

"Thank you, Steve," she replied.

Steve helped put everything in the car, making sure

LOSS OF FAITH

Angela was safe and secure. He was good with her, which made me feel right about going out with him.

Steve had a *Morris Minor* in an aubergine colour that he had souped up. He was into his cars and improving looks and performance.

Angela was busy in the back seat eating her lollypop and playing with her new teddy bear.

"Well, we are off to Sherwood Forest," he said, smiling at me and glancing back at Angela.

"Where is *Sherwood Forest*?" Angela asked without taking her eyes off her new teddy.

"It's in *Nottingham* where *Robin Hood* used to live, Angela. You have watched Robin Hood on television with Mummy, haven't you?" Steve replied.

"Yes. Will we see Robin Hood, Mummy?" Angela asked.

"No, darling, Robin died a long time ago," I replied turning, looking at her and smiling.

"Is that okay with everyone?" Steve asked.

"Yes, that's great!" I said, smiling.

"Are you happy to go to *Sherwood Forest*?" Steve asked looking at her through the rear view mirror.

"Yes!" she replied.

He kept talking all the way to *Sherwood Forest*, keeping us both amused. When we got there, he parked the car and we all got out and went for a walk. There was a play area for the kids. I don't know who the bigger kid was. Steve grabbed her and ran towards the play area. He went on all the rides with Angela and they were both laughing and giggling. It made me so happy that he was interested in my daughter.

LOSS OF FAITH

We sat for a while and had our picnic. Angela chattered away with Steve sharing her food with him, or at least what she did not want to eat. It had been a perfect day and I felt really relaxed and happy. It was good to see Angela having fun too.

The day just flew by and it was beginning to get dusk.

"It's time to go home," Steve said, looking at me.

"I know, let's pack up and go," I replied.

Angela helped put things in our picnic basket. Steve carried the basket as we headed for the car. We all climbed in and headed for home.

It had been a lovely day out and I felt a warm glow and all happy. *But I was dreading what was going to happen when I got home especially with Mother.*

Angela fell asleep in the back of the car while Steve and I talked and laughed all the way home. It was about 10:00 p.m. when we got to my house.

"I have had such a lovely day, do you want to do it again tomorrow?" Steve asked.

"That would be really good. Thanks," I replied.

"I'll pick you up at the same time," he said as he leaned over and kissed me.

My heart was racing with excitement.

He helped me to the door, kissed me and Angela good-night and left.

When I walked in, Mother was sitting in her armchair and had her arms folded. She just looked at me giving me the most filthy stare. Father was sitting in his armchair relaxed. He look at me and winked saying, "You look happy. Did you have a good day?"

"Yes, Father, I did, but I am so very tired. I am going

to see to Angela and go to bed. I am going out with Steve again tomorrow," I replied.

"Did you have a good time, Angela?" Father asked

"Yes, Granddad, we played all day," Angela replied rubbing her eyes as she was tired.

"Come on, Angela, bed time," I said, lifting her from the floor.

"See you all in the morning," I said, looking at my dad.

"Good-night," Father replied.

Mother said nothing.

As I turned my head my eyes caught my mother's eyes and she gave me a look of disapproval but I didn't care and just went upstairs to go to bed.

I could hear Mother and Father talking. "This is not right. She is not even divorced," Mother said.

"Oh, leave it alone, Ada. The girl needs a break and she looks happy for a change. I don't care what people think. It's her life and let her get on with it. So, just watch the television," Father replied.

I didn't care anymore I was looking forward to tomorrow and another day out with Steve.

"Mummy, are we really going out with Steve again tomorrow?" Angela asked as I put her into bed.

"Yes, darling, we are, so get some sleep," I replied looking into her eyes and watching them close. She was so tired. She had had a full day.

I climbed in bed beside her, but could not keep my own eyes open. I felt so happy as I fell asleep.

Chapter Nine

Raphael's Warning

There was a loud bang that woke us up. I jumped out of bed to look through the window but could see nothing. I could just feel that something wasn't right but didn't know what. It didn't feel bad, but I could not put my finger on what it was. Just a feeling.

It was amazing! All that I thought I had lost, was coming back much stronger than before. My hearing was so sharp and clear. I could feel people's emotions much stronger and the mystery of the world was creating a curiosity in my mind. The happier I was, the clearer were my thoughts and images. I could see Spirit again. I was feeling like I was home again and connected to the earth and universe. The world had brighter colours. My dreams were becoming more vivid. I was beginning to experience other dimensions. I wanted to sing again and listen to my music. My soul and my heart were beginning to connect.

Where have I been all this time? Being unhappy has

LOSS OF FAITH

changed me. I was beginning to feel sixteen again. What a wonderful feeling.

I got back into bed with Angela.

"Sing to me, Mummy," she said.

"What shall I sing?" I asked.

"Yesterday," she blurted out.

"Yesterday, all my troubles seemed so far away," I started to sing, watching her beautiful face light up and smile. She had the most amazing smile and laugh. She made me so happy and she was my life. She was the one true being that I truly loved, and well worth all the pain and suffering I had gone through. Nothing had ever made me so happy. As I sang, her eyes gradually closed while she sucked her thumb and with the other hand was twisting her hair. She was so beautiful.

I lay by her side just looking at her. She was so special to me. I loved her so much.

As I lay quietly by her side, the bedroom filled with energy and became very hot. Suddenly, the whole room lit up with all the colours of the rainbow and an overwhelming feeling of love came over me. I felt I was in a different place as though I was in the rainbow.

"We are with you, Patricia. You are home with us where you are meant to be," a voice said.

I felt it touch my heart with love, and floods of tears came streaming down my face. I just could not stop crying. I held my daughter so tightly and fell a sleep with her in my arms.

As morning broke, I woke up with a great sense of peace and happiness. We were going out again and that was a great sense of joy to me.

LOSS OF FAITH

Angela was so excited about going out again.

"Come on, Mummy! Get ready or we will be late!" she said.

"Okay, Angela. I am going as fast as I can," I replied.

She was definitely an old soul. She had old ways of saying things.

After we washed and dressed we went downstairs for breakfast. Father was sitting in the living room.

"Hello, you two. Off out are we?" he said laughing.

"Yes, GrandFather, we are going out with Steve again. Do you want to come?" Angela asked

"No, it's better you and Mummy go," Father replied.

We continued into the kitchen to get breakfast. Mother was washing up and made sure she did not look up or say anything.

"We are going out, Grandma," Angela spouted.

Mother had to look and said, "I know, Angela."

She really did not want to acknowledge it, but she had no choice.

Angela and I had breakfast and I washed up our pots.

"Steve is here, Mummy!" she shouted as she got off her chair and ran to the door.

"Just a minute, Angela," I replied as I dried my hands and got our coats.

I opened the backdoor, letting Angela out.

"We are out for the day, bye," I said.

"Okay. Have a good day," Father replied.

Mother said nothing, as usual.

Steve was playing with Angela as I got to the car.

"Come on, Angela, get in! It's time to go!" Steve said.

She was so excited and not a word said as she clam-

LOSS OF FAITH

bered into the back of the car.

Steve and I got in the car.

"I thought we would go to the country park," he said.

"That would be nice," I replied.

"Is that okay with you, Angela?" Steve asked.

"Yes," she said, her face beaming with the most beautiful smile.

"Okay, that's where we will go then," he said as he started the car and drove off.

"I had a lovely day yesterday," Steve said.

"So did I," I replied.

There was a strong bond building between us.

When we arrived at the country park, there was a fun fair with rides. Steve was like a big kid, so he and Angela got on well. He took her on the bumper cars and waltser. He helped her shoot the frogs and toy people down on the shooting games to get her the big teddy that she wanted. We ate candy floss and toffee apples as well as hotdogs.

It was a day of laughter and fun. I was crying with laughter at both Steve and Angela. The day just seemed to fly by. The sun was setting and it was time to head home.

"Come on you two, it's time to go," I said, looking at the two kids in front of me, one little, one big.

"Shall we do as Mummy says, Angela? What do you think?" Steve asked.

"She will get mad if we don't," Angela replied laughing.

We all climbed into the car and headed for home. Angela was so tired she fell quickly to sleep in the back of the car

On the way back, out of the blue, Steve said, "If you

LOSS OF FAITH

are ever stuck, I have a house you both can stay in, as I live with my mother and the house is empty. I just wanted you to know that."

"Thanks, that is good to know," I replied.

No one had ever made that kind of offer to me, and I had to hold the tears back as it overwhelmed me.

We kept talking and laughing all the way home. The journey flew by. It seemed minutes rather than hours.

When we got there, we were just about to get out of the car when Steve said, "Shall we go out again next Saturday? I can pick you both up and we can go somewhere."

"That would be good," I replied. He kissed me and my heart pounded. He looked me straight in the eyes and I felt my pulse race. I quickly turned away.

"Come on, Angela, it's time to go home," I said, looking at her and nudging her to wake up.

"We have enjoyed our day out. Thank you." I said to Steve as I got Angela out of the car.

"So have I." he replied as he drove off.

I took a big deep breath as I went inside the house with Angela.

I felt I was beaming because my heart was so happy and full of excitement.

"Did you enjoy yourself?" Father asked.

"Yes, we had a lovely time," I replied.

Mother looked serious and muttered something under her breath.

"That's enough, Ada," Father said.

Angela could hardly keep her eyes open, as she had had a long active day.

"I am going to go to bed, as I have to get up to take

LOSS OF FAITH

Angela to play school and go to work tomorrow," I said walking out of the living room and up the stairs.

"Good night, then," Father said, as I closed the stairs door.

"Goodnight, Father," I replied.

I was floating on clouds. I could not stop thinking about Steve.

Angela and I got washed and got into bed. Nothing was said as we were both very tired and couldn't keep our eyes open. But my heart was so happy that I spent more time singing to Angela to get her to sleep. She fell asleep in my arms while holding my hair.

She is such a beautiful and loving child. I could not want for anything else.

In that moment of resting, something beautiful happened. A white light appeared and the Angel Raphael stood there, smiling at me. His robes were green and blue. Such stunning colours and his presence so strong.

"You are a good mother, Patricia," he said.

"I hope so," I replied.

"You have more pain to come, Patricia, but I will be by your side," he said.

"I don't want more pain. I am happy with my daughter and seeing Steve. I am happy. Why would you make me sad?" I questioned.

"You will see," he said as he disappeared into the white light, leaving a total blackness behind.

I fell asleep wondering what on earth it was all about.

Chapter Ten

Up for the Challenge

The alarm clock rang startling me as it went off. It sounded like *Big Ben*. I had been in a deep, deep sleep and I shot up like a bat out of hell thinking I had overslept. I got up with Angela rushing round like a headless chicken to head for play school and work. We had a tight schedule so I could not waste any time. I threw Angela in the bath and flung her clothes on. It was like a whirlwind.

We got to play school. Angela did not want to stay.

"Don't leave me, Mummy," she cried, tears streaming down her face while she was pulling at my hand.

"I have to go to work today, Angela, I am so sorry," I replied.

I dare not look at her as I knew I would weaken to her eyes and tears. I quickly walked into the play school and left her crying with the nun. Angela did not want me to go. I could not look back as I could hear her screaming, "Mummy! Mummy!"

LOSS OF FAITH

That really pulled at my heart. I cried all the way to work and pulled myself together, drying my eyes, taking a deep breathe and putting a smile on my face as I pushed the entrance doors open and entered the reception area at work. There was my boss waiting for me with a smile on his face.

"Come into my office, Patricia," he said.

He walked in front of me and I followed. I was a little nervous as I didn't know what it was all about.

"Sit down Patricia and have a cup of tea with me," he said pouring a cup and placing it down on his desk in front of me.

I sat down saying, "Thank you."

What is this all about?

"Don't look so worried, Patricia. I am making you production manager for the factory," he said, smiling.

"Really?" I said in amazement.

"Yes, are you surprised?" he asked.

"Well, yes. No woman has gotten beyond supervisor," I said.

"I know and it is not going to be easy because the factory manager does not want a woman in this position. But I want you because I know you will do a good job and you have the capabilities to go further. It could get ugly as there are problems in the factory. I want to know that you want to do this because the factory manager has already told me that he will make you fail," he said.

"Well, if you have faith in me, I am certainly up for the challenge," I replied.

"Good," he said, as he handed me a letter, which stated the offer for the position and what I would get paid.

LOSS OF FAITH

"I will need to go to the social security office to give them this letter and sign off," I said.

"Well, do that now and I will prepare the factory manager for when you get back," he replied.

I left and went to sign off the unemployment benefits. My head was buzzing. Someone saw the potential in me.

But what was all that last night with Raphael? Things are going well, not bad.

When I got back to work, the director took me to the factory manager's office and introduced me.

"This is Patricia," Mr. Mays, the director, said to the factory manager.

"Patricia, this is Steve, the factory manager."

I had not met him before. He was Welsh, with a balding head and a pot belly.

He looked down at me over his glasses and said, "I hope you are fully aware, that I do not want a woman in this job, especially you, as you have come through the director, and I will make you fail," he snapped.

"Yes, I know how you feel, but I don't care. You will eat your words and have to apologize to me in six month's time, as I won't let you make me fail," I replied.

Mr. Mays, the director, stood watching for a while and then left smiling.

No one is going to say that to me and get away with it. I know where I stand and I will show him.

"You can go and work with the skirt section as we have major problems with quality and production targets. We have a visit in three weeks from our customer and if we do not get it right, we will lose the business. So let's see what you can do with that. Everyone else has tried and

LOSS OF FAITH

failed. So let's see what you are made of," he said.

"Okay, let's just see," I replied, leaving his office and heading for the skirt section.

I introduced myself to the supervisors and quality people and spent the first few hours walking with them and talking to the people to find out what was going wrong. I made notes to look back on. Then, I left them, went to my office and sat down working out the work flow and a list of jobs and timings. I then got the supervisors and the quality people together to work out who was best for the job and where we needed to train. We came up with a plan that we would implement in the morning. It was the supervisor's job to inform people what was happening and who was doing what.

Time passed quickly and it was time to go. As I was walking out of the building the factory manager said sarcastically, "I see you have wasted time talking and not doing any improvements today."

"Well, you may think that but let's wait and see what happens tomorrow when I implement my plan, shall we?" I replied, just walking past him.

I was so mad, but determined.

The arrogant pig.

I rushed over to play school, picked up Angela, who was pleased to see me, and headed for home. I was tired as it had been a long day.

"What have you been doing today, Angela?" I asked.

"Drawing and playing games, Mummy and I have my new friend, Amy," She replied.

She seemed happy and that made me feel happy. I was so worried that she would hate it.

LOSS OF FAITH

"That's good, Angela. You will be able to play with Amy tomorrow," I said.

"Yes, Mummy," she replied.

We arrived home and walked into the kitchen where Father was having his dinner. Mother was standing at the kitchen sink washing the pots. Father smiled and Mother just looked at me with dismay.

"How did your first day go, Patricia?" Father asked.

"Oh, interesting, to say the least," I replied.

After explaining the day's events to him, he said, "Well, I know you will make it good."

"Oh, I know so. I am not going to let that pig of a man win. He will eat his words," I replied.

"How did you like play school, Angela?" Father asked.

"I have a new friend called Amy, and we played games together," Angela replied all excited.

"Come and sit on my knee and tell me all about it," Father said.

Angela climbed up and never stopped chattering.

I quickly got something to eat for both of us. Angela ate her dinner while sitting on Father's knee, both of them enjoying talking, laughing and eating. Angela made sure Father shared her dinner.

"I am going to spend some time with Angela and then go to bed as I am tired," I said, as I stood up picked up Angela and left the kitchen to go upstairs.

"Okay. You look tired, see you tomorrow," Father said.

Mother never said a word.

I played with Angela for a while, drawing and read-

LOSS OF FAITH

ing *Cinderella*. She loved fairy stories. I wanted to be able to give her some time so she felt secure even though I was getting sleepy myself.

I felt happy because her school was a worry to me. I wanted to work but I also wanted her to be happy.

"Come on, Angela, it's time for a bath and then we can go to bed to sleep," I said.

"Am I going back to school and Amy tomorrow?" she asked.

"Yes, you are going back tomorrow," I replied.

We got into the bath together playing water fights and then got dried and dressed and climbed into bed.

"Sing me a song, Mummy," she giggled.

I looked at her amazing eyes that were so full of love and understanding.

"What shall I sing," I asked.

"Ba-ba Black Sheep," she replied.

I started singing and watched her eyes gently close. I just lay there looking at her. She was so beautiful and I fell asleep with that picture in my mind.

That night I started dreaming again. I saw my daughter in distress and I was running after her. As I woke up beads of sweat were pouring from my body, I felt fearful and in panic. This was the only bit of my dream that I remembered. I got hold of Angela and held her so tight. I was so scared at the very thought I would lose her.

I wonder what that is all about as I am happy and my daughter is happy.

I could not get back to sleep. I lay awake feeling knots tightening in my stomach and my heart just pounding like a drum, that bit of my dream playing over and over in

LOSS OF FAITH

my head, tears flowing down my face with despair. I just could not bear the thought of losing Angela. I held her so tight as I watched the darkness of the night disappear and the dawn gradually break through the window. The darkness had seemed endless, my mind on a roller coaster of torment and torture, my heart filled with so much fear and sadness.

Chapter Eleven

Bedroom Time Travel

The rest of the week followed the same routine: getting Angela to play school and me to my office. I implemented my plan at work and by the end of the week, the work was flowing, targets were met, the section was profitable and the quality of the product was exceptional.

On Friday afternoon, before I left, I had a meeting with the factory manager and director.

"Well done, Patricia, I knew you could do it. Now, the section is working well. We have brought the customer's visit forward to next Friday and we want you to handle that visit. Is that all right with you?" the director asked.

"That's fine. We can talk on Monday to let me know what is required, and I will sort it out for Friday," I replied.

I looked at the factory manager. "Have you nothing to say to me?" I asked.

"No, it was just luck," he replied.

"We will see. I am off now to pick up my daughter

LOSS OF FAITH

from play school," I said, leaving the building with a big smug smile on my face.

I did it and he didn't like it.

It had been a hard week and I was tired but at the same time, I was looking forward to seeing Steve over the weekend.

I picked Angela up and we headed for home.

"Have you had a good day at play school?" I asked.

"Yes, Mummy. I have been playing with my friend and drawing and reading a story," she replied.

"What story?" I enquired.

"*Pinocchio,*" she replied.

"And what did you draw?" I asked.

"A new home for us and a garden," she replied.

"That's nice. Are we getting a new home?" I asked.

"Yes, Mummy," she replied with excitement in her voice.

"Are we seeing Steve this weekend?" she enquired.

"Yes, sweetheart, we are. Why?" I asked.

"I like Steve," she said.

"I am glad to hear that," I replied.

That makes me feel good. It's important that they get on and like each other. I like him too.

My mother and father had gone out, so we landed home to a quiet and empty house. It was late, so we had something to eat and went to bed as we had a busy weekend ahead.

The weekend was really good, spending Saturday and Sunday out with Steve and Angela. We all had a great time.

When I got home on Sunday night my mother and

father were watching television. I sat down in the chair with Angela, and my father said, "Your mother and I have been talking and we want to help you. During the week, I can pick Angela up from play school so you can work full time, and on a Saturday night, when we get back from church, we will baby sit Angela for you as long as you are back home by 10:30 p.m."

I was dumbfounded.

Where did this come from?

"Did you hear what I said?" Father asked.

"Yes, I did and thank you," I replied.

"Well you look tired and we want to help don't we, Mother?" he asked.

"Yes," she said quietly.

I ran up to my father and gave him a big hug.

"That's enough. I am watching television," Mother snapped, obviously not happy with what my father had said.

I knew it was my father and not my mother, who had instigated this. She did not want to help me. I sensed it.

But I knew that Father had put his foot down. I did not care who, what, or why. I just wanted to do full time work and get out one night a week.

"I am tired, so I am going to bed," I said, as I went upstairs with Angela.

When I had sung her to sleep, I sat there thinking.

What a week and in such a short time everything can change.

I was so happy that I had the chance to turn my life around. But, I also had this feeling of being frightened about being happy. If it all went wrong, that happiness

LOSS OF FAITH

was just a fleeting glimpse of nothing.

I could hear Mother and Father talking downstairs. Father was definitely getting it in the neck for helping me out.

At this point, I did not care what Mother thought. My happiness mattered more than anything and so did Angela's. I gave her one last hug and rolled over to go to sleep. I could sense movement in the room and some sort of light. My heart started racing and I wanted to scream but could not make a sound. I plucked up the courage to turn and have a look. I just could not believe what I was seeing.

The bedroom wall disappeared and a whole dimensional shift occurred. Where the wall had been, a scene from the 1800's appeared, with carts and horses and people carrying hay and all sorts of goods. It seemed to be a shabby one-road town. The road was just soil and as the carts and horses drove by, dust from the road floated in the air like a thick mist. There were old buildings made of wood and a little town with its little stores, selling clothes and food and a church to the end of the street. I could smell fresh bread baking. There was a smell of age and staleness. The wind whipped up the dust from the road making my throat dry. The women wore long dresses and the men wore trousers , shirts, jackets and hats. It seemed a polite time as the men tipped their hats to the ladies and said, "Good morning," as they walked by. There did not seem to be a lot of money about as everyone's clothes were a bit tattered and worn. I rubbed my eyes to make sure I was seeing what I thought I was seeing, and it was still there. I quickly picked up Angela and held her very tightly.

You are not having my daughter, too.

LOSS OF FAITH

"We don't want your daughter. We are connecting with you, and bringing you back home," a voice said.

"I won't leave my daughter," I said quickly, scared that this was what I had been dreaming about.

"No, Patricia, we don't want any of that. We just want to reconnect with you because you are changing. We can talk to you again and help you," someone said.

I smiled and said, "I am talking to myself."

"Why would you think that? Can you not see the dimensional shift in front of your eyes? This is all real. Talk to the people and see what happens," a voice said.

"But, who are you?" I asked.

"We are the Atlanteans, from the lost city of Altantis," someone replied.

"What do you want?" I asked.

At this point, a woman from the dimensional shift looked straight at me, smiled and said, "Hello, Patricia."

"You, know me?" I asked, with a quizzical look.

"Of course I do. We have seen each other many times," the woman said.

"Where have you seen me?" I asked, my voice quivering and a sense of fear beginning to rise.

"In Atlantis many years ago. You are one of us and there is no need to be afraid Patricia," she replied in a calm voice.

"You can sense my fear?" I asked.

"Yes, I can, just like you can sense things," she replied.

This is freaky.

"No, it's not. Telepathic communication is our way," a voice said.

"It is time for us to work with you and further develop you. We will be back," a voice said.

"You can hear my thoughts?" I said with a puzzled look on my face.

"Yes, that is as normal for us as it is for you. There is much to learn Patricia. Just wait and see," she replied.

As she was talking to me I was getting flash backs to a city that was filled with radiant sunshine where people were in simple flowing outfits of white. The atmosphere was very calm and happy. People talked to each other but in their heads, like an advanced race of beings. I could see lots of light and crystals glowing in the sunshine.

As quickly as everything had appeared, it disappeared and my bedroom was back to normal.

I hung onto my daughter with all my might, as no one was going to take her away from me. My head was spinning.

Could this be what my dream means?

I could not get this out of my mind.

Is this real?

My stomach tied into knots from my fear of losing my daughter. Everything was just repeating in my head and I felt panic taking over my body. I was holding my daughter so tight. The room was so dark and I felt so scared. The night just seemed so long. I could only hear the clock ticking.

Suddenly, my eyes became heavy and my thoughts started drifting until I fell asleep.

Chapter Twelve

Dresses, Trousers & Playschool

Monday morning came and I got ready to take Angela to play school. I had a busy week ahead of me at work, but first, I needed to sort out arrangements for Father to pick up Angela.

When we got to play school, I asked to see the manager, Mrs. Burns. She was in her early 40's with long greying hair tied back in a pony tail. She was a slim lady but dressed a bit like Miss Marples— blue checked skirt to her calf and a grey jacket with a white long sleeved blouse underneath and dark blue court shoes. As she came out of her office, she took short steps and walked quickly as though there was no time to lose. She always walked this way.

"What can I do for you Patricia?" she asked with hesitation in her voice.

"There is nothing majorly wrong, Mrs. Burns. I just wanted to notify you about what was happening and that the only people that Angela should be released to is me or my father," I replied as I quickly pulled out a photograph of my father and handed it to her.

"This is a picture of my father. You can keep in on file so everyone can see what he looks like. You understand what is going on with Angela's father so I don't want any mistakes. My father will start picking her up tonight," I quickly said.

"That's fine, Patricia. I will notify all the staff and show them the picture. Don't worry, everything will be fine," Mrs. Burns replied.

"Thank you. I will take Angela to her playgroup," I said as I turned and walked to the playroom.

"You are welcome," Mrs. Burns said as she walked to her office.

I led Angela into the playroom, took off her coat and hung it on the hangers on the wall.

"Give me a kiss, Angela, and don't forget your grand-dad is picking you up tonight and I will see you at his house," I said as I bent down giving her a hug and a kiss.

"Okay, Mummy. I will see you later," she replied as she ran off full of excitement to play with her friends.

I left the play school and headed for work, trying not to be late. I just about ran all the way there.

When I arrived I was out of breath. No sooner than I had taken my coat off, I was called into a meeting with the director and factory manager.

Still out of breath, I rushed over to the director's office.

"You look flustered, Patricia," the director said.

"No, I've just been rushing around dropping off my

LOSS OF FAITH

daughter at play school," I replied as I sat down.

"Well, we have a lot of work to do for the visit this Friday from are customers. This is so important to us. If we lose the business, then jobs will have to go," the director said.

"What products are they coming to look at?" I asked.

"Dresses, skirts and trousers," he replied.

"In other words, they will end up looking at everything," I said.

"Afraid so," the director said.

"So, how are the other sections performing?" I asked.

"Not as bad as the skirt section you have just done," the factory manager said.

"So why are we sitting here? Let's go and do some work," I said.

"I told you she was a little dynamo," the director said.

I have four days to knock this into shape.

I went home that evening feeling tired but concerned to know whether Father had picked up Angela. All had gone well and according to plan. When I got home and walked through the back door, there was Angela sitting at the kitchen table with Mother and Father having dinner. The relief I felt inside took all my anxieties away in a split second. She had been on my mind all day and I really hoped that all would go well.

"Mummy, Granddad came and picked me up and drove me home," Angela said filled with excitement.

"I know darling. Did you like that?"

"Yes, Mummy. I love Granddad," she said.

Angela was chattering away to Mother and Father while I got myself something to eat. I was so tired I left them all to it. After we had finished dinner I looked at Angela saying, "It's time for bed, Angela."

"Mummy..." she replied.

"No, Angela, it's bed time and no arguments," I said.

"You look very tired, Patricia," Father said, looking at me and smiling.

"Yes, Father, I am. So I am off to bed," I said getting up and taking Angela upstairs.

It had been a long day, so it was a quick bath for both of us and we went to bed.

"Sing me a song, Mummy," Angela said laughing.

"Okay," I replied.

Ba Ba Black Sheep was the favourite this week, and while I was singing, I watched her eyes fall heavy and soon she fell asleep. I was not far behind her.

The next few days were very busy. In fact, I worked like a dog, non-stop, and by Thursday night, everything was done. The lines were performing to quality and performance targets. The samples were done and everything was set up for our customers visit the following morning. They usually came early to make sure nothing was hidden. But, I was happy with what I had achieved and definitely ready for their visit.

"You have done well, Patricia," the director said.

"I owe you an apology, Patricia," the factory manager said.

Both the director and I turned to look at him.

He was a bit embarrassed, and said, "You are amazing at what you do. I could not have a better production manager working for me. I am sorry I made that judgment

LOSS OF FAITH

when you first got the position. I hope we can put it all behind us and have a good working relationship."

"I think when the visit is over tomorrow, you can take the three of us out to the pub for a bite to eat and a drink to celebrate a job well done. Then, all this can be put behind us," I replied, laughing.

"Okay, you have a deal," he replied.

We all headed out of the factory to go our separate ways home. I was really tired and needed to get some sleep to be ready for the visit the following day.

Friday came, and the customers turned up at 8:00 a.m., but I was ready for them. A man and a woman, both about the same age in their fifties with grey hair, both in suits and carrying briefcases. They could have been twins as they resembled each other in looks, dress, and mannerisms. I watched them walk through the reception door and towards the factory manager who had already met them before.

As they approached us, Steve, the factory manager said, "This is Patricia, our new production manager, and Patricia, this is Mrs. May and Mr. Duncan."

"Pleased to meet you both," I quickly said, holding out my hand to shake theirs.

"We have heard very good reports about you, Patricia," Mr. Duncan said, shaking my hand and smiling.

We seemed to hit it off straight away.

"We would like Patricia to do this visit with us if you don't mind, Steve," Mrs. May said.

"No, that is fine by me," Steve replied with a sigh of relief on his face.

They seemed to want to stay with me, so he just

tagged along. I got on really well with them and was able to express my opinions about the buttons they had provided, that were too soft. They stayed about four hours. It was a very good visit and they seemed very happy when I dropped them back at the Director's office.

"Goodbye, Mrs. May and Mr. Duncan. Have a safe journey and it was really good to meet you," I said, smiling.

"Thank you too, Patricia. It has been a good, interesting and informative day with you. We will see you again soon," Mrs. May said.

I closed the door as I left and walked back into the factory.

About thirty minutes later the director called both the factory manager and me into his office. He had a big smile on his face as we both walked in.

"Our customers were extremely impressed with you, Patricia," he said.

"Why was that?" I enquired.

"You were honest with them and knew what you were talking about. They liked your honesty and they want to make sure you do all the visits with them," he replied.

"Well, I would be happy to do them, if it's okay with everyone," I replied.

"I am happy for you to do them. I hate doing customer visits," the factory manager said.

"Well, let's go and eat at your expense then," I said, laughing.

We all left for the pub where we sat, ate, talked and just relaxed. It had been a hard week but we had reaped rewards for the company. More work was to come.

Chapter Thirteen

Five Minutes, a Slap & Merlin

The weekend came and I was looking forward to seeing Steve again. While Angela and I were with Steve, I got to spend some time alone with him, which was good.

Father had had words with Mother and she had agreed to look after Angela, so Steve and I could go out for something to eat on Saturday night. I know Father was fed up of seeing me unhappy and was trying to do his best for me. It was a miracle that Mother had agreed, but I was happy with the outcome. We went to the steak house in Doncaster and had a lovely evening. After the meal, we went back to Steve's place to watch a film but we fell asleep. I suddenly woke up. It was 10:25 p.m. and I had to be in by 10:30 p.m. I woke up Steve and we rushed to get home as quickly as possible.

I landed home at 10:35 p.m. "I am in trouble now," I said to Steve.

"You are only five minutes late," he replied.

LOSS OF FAITH

"Oh, no, this is World War Three. See you tomorrow," I said to Steve, as I got out of the car.

"Here are the keys to my house. If there is any problem, move in and I will be at my mother's house," Steve said as he kissed me good night.

"Thank you, that is so good of you," I replied as I slipped the keys into my handbag and got out of the car.

My heart was pounding. I could feel the anger as I walked down the path to the back door. I opened it and went in. There was Mother, with her finger already wagging at me, as she said, "You are late."

"Mother, I am five minutes late. I am tired and want to go to bed," I replied.

But, I could not get upstairs. Mother was not going to let it rest. She was going on and on and on until I could not take it any more. I grabbed her arm and pulled her out of the doorway.

"Bob are you going to stand there and let her do this to me?" she screamed.

Father jumped up and tried to calm everyone down, but by this time, everything was out of hand. Mother was screaming at both of us. I answered back rudely, and then, suddenly, Father hit me straight across the face. That shocked me because he had never hit me before. I just stood there speechless for a couple of seconds. It seemed like a lifetime.

"That's it. I am out of here tomorrow. I am not staying in this house another day. I will pack up and leave in the morning," I said, storming off to bed.

My heart was pounding and I burst into tears.

Finally, Mother has managed to turn my father against me.

LOSS OF FAITH

I hated my mother for getting what she wanted.

I had it all planned. Steve had said that I could stay at his place and he would stay at his mother's. I could not sleep as my thoughts were of my father hitting me. All I could do was cry. Angela was sound asleep. I tossed and turned thinking

What about Angela? I cannot keep moving her about, but if we are to be happy, I have to leave and live at Steve's so we can have a life.

I could not drop to sleep. My mind was racing and my heart was in so much pain I could feel the palpitations and panic setting in. I watched the dawn break and I felt so sad. I love my dad, but I knew I could not stay any longer under the same roof as my mother.

Angela woke up rubbing her eyes with her hands.

"Mummy, have you been crying?" she asked, looking at my face.

I must have looked like an absolute wreck to her.

"No, Angela. I just have not been well in the night, that's all," I quickly replied.

"We have lots to do this morning, Angela," I said waiting for a response.

"What are we doing, Mummy?" she asked.

"We have to pack all our things and we are going to live at Steve's house. Would you like that?" I asked.

"Yes, Mummy. Is Steve going to be there?" she asked.

"No, sweetheart, but he will visit us," I replied.

We got up and washed and dressed and Angela helped me pack our things.

"You stay here while I take things downstairs," I said.

"Okay, Mummy," she replied.

LOSS OF FAITH

I carried our bags downstairs and went back to get Angela.

There was complete silence. You could hear a pin drop as I walked through to the kitchen.

"We are going to live in a new house," Angela said, all excited.

"That will be nice," Father said.

They could ignore me but they could not ignore Angela.

I grabbed some breakfast for Angela and me, went into the room to get our things.

Father followed me into the room. "Are you sure you want to do this, Patricia?" he asked.

"I am sure. I cannot stay another day in this house. I am twenty-two years old and I was five minutes late. Have you never fallen asleep because you were tired? I am not a child, Father. I am all grown up, living under Mother's rules or else. That's not me, Father. I can't stay here," I replied.

"Where are you going?" he enquired.

"Steve is going to let me stay at his place and he will be living at his mother's house," I said.

"Are you going to be okay?" Father asked.

"Yes, I will," I replied, giving him a hug.

"I will still pick Angela up from play school and bring her here for you to pick her up," he said.

"Thanks, Father, that will be a help," I replied.

At that moment, Steve turned up to take us out for the day. I carried all of our things to the car.

"Are you all right?" he asked.

"Yes, I am. It was a volcano erupting last night. So,

LOSS OF FAITH

I am taking you up on your offer to stay at your place," I said.

"That's fine. We can go and drop things off first and then, have a cup of tea," he replied.

Here I am moving again.

I was not feeling very talkative as I hated falling out with my father. I know I had hurt him by leaving, but I could not stand to live with my mother any longer.

Steve knew I did not want to talk, so he played with Angela, making her laugh and giggle, to give me some space.

"Mum and Dad said they would baby sit for you, if we wanted to go out tonight," Steve said.

"Yes, that would be nice. I would like that," I replied.

We went out and had a good time. I made an effort on the outside, although on the inside, my stomach was churning and full of knots.

Steve took me home to pick up his mum and dad.

We walked down the path and through the back door into the living room where Steve's mum and dad were watching television.

"Have you had a good time?" Steve's dad asked looking at me.

"Yes, thank you," I replied.

He was a tall, bald, stocky man. He was retired and was missing a thumb and little finger from an accident he had many years ago. They had Steve late in life. But his father was a nice man. His mother was a small petite lady with gray hair. She was born with a club foot and wore special shoes. She was a lovely lady.

"Thank you for babysitting. Has Angela been good?"

LOSS OF FAITH

"That's all right, Patricia. Angela is such a lovely little girl and she has been good. It has been a pleasure to babysit," Steve's dad replied, and his mother smiled at me.

His parents were really lovely people and I know they liked me. I could feel it.

"Well, son, it's time for us to go home," his dad said, getting up.

His mother got up saying, "You say goodnight to Patricia and we will wait by the car."

"Okay, Mother," he replied.

"Goodnight Patricia," they both said as they gave me a hug before leaving.

"Goodnight," I replied.

They left and Steve kissed me.

"Are you going to be okay?" Steve asked.

"I will be fine, don't worry," I replied.

"Okay, I will call round tomorrow," he said.

"Okay, that will be good," I said walking him to the door.

He stepped out of the back door, turned to look at me and blew me a kiss.

I closed and locked the door to spend my first night in my new place. I leaned against the door thinking

This is my first night on my own in my new home.

There was stillness in the house. You could hear a pin drop. It was peaceful.

In this house, Angela had her own bedroom so I went in to see if she was all right. She was fast asleep cuddling a big brown teddy bear that Steve's parents had bought her. She was so beautiful and looked so cute. All I could do was smile. This meant a new start for both of us.

LOSS OF FAITH

I got washed, changed and got into bed.

I just lay there, listening to the silence, letting my mind drift slowly into sleep. I could feel my spirit leaving my body. I looked down to see myself lying so still.

Things were beginning to happen again. As I looked around the room, a white light appeared and through it, came Merlin.

"It's good to be back, Patricia," he said, stroking his beard.

"It's good to see you again, Merlin," I replied.

"I have come to take you travelling to show you things. Are you ready to go?" he asked.

"Yes, I am," I replied.

He took my hand, turned, and we walked into the white light. We travelled into the past and into the future. Travelling with Merlin was always exciting watching time pass by before your eyes. It was like fast forwarding a video. We went to the future first. That was confusing for me as I did not understand—towering buildings, lots of glass and steel. Everything appeared stiff and rigid. Everyone sat at desks glued to what looked like small television screens and typing. There seemed to be no conversations or interaction. Everything was clean, spick and span, with nothing out of place. It gave off such a cold and isolated feeling. There were robots walking about taking things here and there. I didn't like it here. I now know the TV screens were computers. The people were more like robots just looking at the screens and typing. They were not speaking or interacting. It felt like such a sad time.

"Can we go from here Merlin. I don't like it here it's so cold, clinical and isolating," I said.

LOSS OF FAITH

"Yes, Patricia, but this is the future," he replied, as he turned, holding my hand. Time started going backwards, scenes of the Industrial Revolution, wars, and poverty until we landed in *Camelot*. Everything took my breath away, but I loved *Camelot*—the old castle, the round table and King Arthur and the knights. We were in the big hall and everyone was eating, drinking and laughing. King Arthur sat at the top table with his family. The knights and the courtiers sat at the side tables. The tables were overflowing with food. The servants topping everyone's goblets with wine. Jugglers were performing in the centre of the room. Everyone was happy. There was always a stale unhealthy smell to *Camelot*, but it was an exciting period in time for me and I felt at home. I didn't want to leave. It always made me feel so happy. The future was very confusing, as I did not know what it all meant. So I asked questions, as I was curious.

"What is the future all about?" I asked.

"You will understand later," Merlin said.

"Why can't I know now?" I asked.

"There is no real value in knowing right now. So, later, Patricia. It's just a journey right now," he replied.

He wouldn't tell me anything about the future. Merlin was such a character. It was always good to be with him and I enjoyed our journeys.

"Well, Patricia, it's time to go back, and we'll do this again," he said.

"I know. Bye Merlin," I replied.

At that very second, everything went black.

I woke up the next morning full of life, as though my body had renewed itself. That was the only way I could explain it.

LOSS OF FAITH

I felt light, almost glowing, as I got Angela ready for play school and myself ready for work. I was singing under my breath.

Yes, the old me is coming out again.

"Do you like your new home, Angela?" I asked.

"Yes, Mummy. I have my own bedroom," she replied.

I dropped Angela off at play school and headed for work. I felt so much lighter. It was like walking on air. When I got to work, everyone commented on how different I was.

Where has all this come from. I only travelled with Merlin, but I can't say anything to anyone as they would think I am mad.

So, I just smiled and accepted their comments.

The next couple of weeks were pretty much the same. I saw much more of Steve than before, and I went to collect Angela from Father's place after work. Everything seemed to be working out perfectly, until one day...

Chapter Fourteen

Losing Angela, Losing Control

I got up with this really bad feeling in the pit of my stomach. So much so that I felt sick and filled with an awful anxiety that was doing my head in.

I wonder what this could be about.

I knew I was not ill. I could tell this was something that was going to happen but what, I did not know. My head was running through all the permutations it could be possibly be.

But Angela and I were happy in our new home and everything was going okay. Was it my mother or father or my sister and brother?

Round and round my thoughts swirled, but I could find no answers. I had such a bad feeling and I had learnted to listen as it always had a meaning. I had to try and push it to one side as I had things to do.

I dropped my daughter off at play school and gave her a big hug. As I held her, she said, "Mummy, I love you."

LOSS OF FAITH

"I love you too. See you tonight," I replied, giving her another hug, and then I left for work.

All day I was tense, getting palpitations and anxiety attacks. I could not explain it. I was glad when work came to an end and I could go home.

I caught the bus and set off to Father's place to pick up Angela. As I walked down the drive, I felt like someone had driven a knife through my heart. I ran to the door and flung it open.

"Where is Angela?" I asked frantically, as I looked in all the rooms.

"Come and sit down, Patricia, and let me explain," Father said.

"Where is she? Is she hurt? Is she in the hospital? She is my daughter," I cried.

"Someone has taken Angela from school. It was not Trevor, but another man," Father said, trying to calm me down with his words and calm tone of voice.

"I told them and wrote them a letter, not to let anyone take her, except you and me," I cried, rushing to the door.

"Where are you going Patricia?" Father asked, getting up and rushing to stop me from leaving the house. He got hold of me and turned me around and put his arms around me, holding me tight. I was in sheer panic and tears were flooding from my eyes. I could hardly get my breath from sobbing.

"I am going to Trevor's Mum's shop. That's where she will be," I said, pulling away from my Father, pushing passed him and stomping out the back door.

"Hang on, Patricia I will drive you there," Father said, grabbing his car keys and rushing after me.

LOSS OF FAITH

Father opened the car doors and we both got in. I sat in the car not saying a word. I was filled with overwhelming emotion and pain. Someone had not only stuck a knife in my heart, but had twisted it around and around. The pain was so bad, I could hardly breathe. I just did not know what I would do without Angela. The very thought made me feel I did not want to live.

Father parked the car at the side of the shop. We got out and walked through the front door. It had an old fashioned single bell that made one tingling sound as you opened the shop door. It was an end terraced house converted into a shop. There was a long counter and the glass door fridge freezers were to the side on the right. The electric meat slicers were to the left of the counter. All the stock was on old shelves attached to the walls. The door to the living quarters was right in the centre of the wall at the back of the counter and had a beaded blind that made a rattling sound as his mother and father walked in. There was only me and my father in the shop facing his parents.

"Where is my daughter?" I asked.

"Don't know. She is not here. Have you lost her? Well, that does not surprise us," Trevor's mother said sarcastically.

"I want my daughter back. I know you sick bastards have taken her because you could not have a daughter of your own, so you want mine. Where is she?" I demanded, heading for the counter.

"Come on, Patricia, you are not going to get anywhere today. Go see the police tonight and the solicitor tomorrow," Father said, pulling me step by step away from the counter and out the door. I didn't want to go as I just wanted my daughter and I knew they had her. I just knew.

"I'll get you for this," I shouted as my Father closed the shop door in my face so I could not say anymore.

"Come on, Patricia, let's get in the car," Father said calmly.

I did not feel calm. The loss of my daughter was like a red rag to a bull. I was angry, nearly out of my head with absolute rage. I could not think straight. Father walked in front to open the car door. He did not know there was a side door to the shop. As he walked ahead, my temper was ready to explode. My heart was racing as I came to the side door of the shop. I just saw red. I turned and like the Incredible Hulk, kicked in the door. There were all of Trevor's brothers, his father and his mother, standing at the back.

"You are not going to get her back," Trevor's father said.

"Really? We will see about that," I said in anger, glaring, my stare piercing through him.

At that point, I did see red, like an animal, watching its prey. I looked at all of them. His mother was laughing. The noise was building up inside my head until I just went for it. Trevor's brother went down first, with one punch. I flung his father across the room, and there, in front of me, was his mother. I wanted to kill her. I had the strength of twenty men. I do not know where the strength came from, but I felt like a mad man, outraged and uncontrollable.

I dragged her down to the floor and was hitting and punching her. I just could not stop myself. I was like a woman possessed. Nothing could stop me. I was in another place, where nothing mattered. I could see myself,

LOSS OF FAITH

and it was as if I was watching it happen in slow motion. However, the most frightening thing was that I just could not stop myself from doing what I was doing.

Chapter Fifteen

A Knife in My Heart

Suddenly, I heard my father's voice and could see his hands on my hands. They were full of blood.

"Come on, Patricia, we are going home," he said, pulling me off Trevor's mother and dragging me out of the shop to the car. He was gripping my hands so tightly I could not move them. I was hysterical, screaming, shouting, "I haven't finished with her yet!"

"That's enough!" he shouted as he let go of one hand and slapped me hard across my face. He then opened the car door and threw me in the car and locked the door so I couldn't get out. I was banging my bloody hands on the car window shouting, "Let me out! Let me out"

He unlocked the driver's door and got in and locked the doors quickly so I couldn't get out. He leaned over grabbing my hands and holding them down as he pulled me away from the window and towards him.

I could not stop crying and sobbing. "They have my

LOSS OF FAITH

Angela! They have my daughter, Father!" I cried.

"I know, Patricia, but we have to do this properly to get her back. Not like this," he calmly replied. "Come on, we are going home," he said.

By this time, people had come out of there terraced houses to stand on the street corner to see what was happening. Crowds of people had gathered together. Everyone was chattering, pointing and looking horrified as though a murder had been committed.

As I looked out of my side window, it was covered in blood. There were lots of hand prints and the blood was running down the window.

"What have I done?"

I got my coat sleeve and wiped as much of the blood off the window as I could, so Father could see. I just stared at the people. I wanted to shout, "What are you looking at?" but I couldn't. I was so numb and exhausted. I could only just stare out of the car window as my father drove off. It was as though I was in a trance watching everything in slow motion.

If Father had not stopped me, I would have killed her. I totally lost it and was out of control. I don't know what I would have done without Father's help.

The pain of losing Angela was unbearable. My head was spinning and my mind replaying everything. It was like I was physically there, but my head was in a different place, hearing everything in the distance. I felt I was standing back, watching myself, and not being able to stop it.

The pain I felt in my heart was overwhelming. All I knew was that I had been in a place where my head had flipped into a different reality where I had no control over what was happening. I never, ever again want to be in that place again.

"I just want my daughter back," I cried.

"I know. We will see the solicitor in the morning, " Father replied.

By this time, I just stared into thin air. Inside I was crying a flood of tears, but no sound was coming out. Just streams of tears flooding down my face as I spoke with my mind to the invisible beings around me.

So, this is what you had planned for me? I knew there was something, but I never believed you could be so mean and hurtful. I do not want anything ever to do with you again. So, go away, and leave me alone for good. You bastards! I hate you. Don't ever come near me again. There is no God, angels or spirit.

My pain and heartache were so severe. I just did not want to live without my daughter.

When we got back to Father's house, he talked to mother, and then phoned the doctor and then, Steve, to let him know what had happened. Mother remained silent but I knew what she was thinking. I could hear her thoughts:

How embarrassing and what will the neighbours think. She is so much trouble.

But I didn't care anymore. I did not want her anywhere near me.

Steve came hurtling down to Father's house and got there, just before the doctor arrived. He hugged me so tight I could hardly breathe. No words were spoken between us.

The doctor turned up and talked to my father, and then he checked me out and gave me a sedative for the night, with a comment that I must go and see him the fol-

LOSS OF FAITH

lowing day.

Everything was in the background. I could hear Steve talking to my Father, but it sounded like they were standing in a tunnel. Here, but not here. I heard Steve say he would take me home and look after me. Father helped me to Steve's car and we set off for the house. I could not talk. It felt like I was in a trance, watching things happen before me, but not feeling that I was a part of anything. All I could think of was that I had lost my daughter.

When we got back to the house, Steve put me to bed and came and sat with me. He kept talking to me and holding me, but I could not answer. I just stared into space until I finally fell asleep. My dreams had become my own nightmare.

I got up the next day, feeling numb from the pain. I was doing all the right things, but like a robot.

I phoned the solicitor who said he would start legal proceedings. I just needed to come in and sign the forms, which I did, with Steve's help. Then I made a visit to the doctor's office, and he put me on tranquilizers.

About tea time, the police landed at the door to interview me, because Trevor's mother had filed a complaint. They could see what state I was in. Steve never moved from my side. They had interviewed my Father before they came to see me.

I told them what had happened and signed the statement. The policeman spoke to Steve and said, "Nothing will come of this, as she was provoked, so, there is nothing to worry about. Let her know that we had to follow up on the complaint. I will make my report and recommendations. She will be fine."

LOSS OF FAITH

I could hear it all, but felt that I was floating by.

Steve had phoned my boss at work and he came to visit me in the evening to bring flowers and see how I was. He did not stay long. He just said, "Take as long as you need off work, Patricia," and he left.

I just cried and cried. All I wanted was to get Angela back. I really was not much use to anyone.

The solicitor came out to see me a week later, and Steve and Father were there.

"Your husband has disappeared with your daughter, so we can't serve the papers on him, "he said. "We have put a private detective on the case to find him, and we will. Until then, there is nothing we can do. I am so sorry, Patricia, but I will let you know as soon as I hear something," he said, and then, he left.

Oh no! It felt like my heart had been ripped from my body. "Why did this have to happen to me?" I screamed. "I want my daughter back – doesn't anyone understand?"

I cried, and my emotions welled up to the surface like a volcano. Father grabbed hold of me and held me tight.

"I know, Patricia, I know," he said.

"The legal system has to be followed to do this properly, but it will be sorted out," Steve said.

I could not get rid of the pain in my heart. I missed Angela so much. I was so frightened that I would never see her again. Day by day my emotions stabilised but my fears remained.

I hope my daughter is okay and being looked after. I love her so much.

My face had been set in concrete and the stress was showing on my face. No one left me alone. Steve and his

LOSS OF FAITH

mum and Father made sure of that. They all helped me with the house work and shopping and tried to keep me busy even though I was not talkative. They made their presence felt and made sure I wouldn't do anything stupid. I just couldn't say much. It was as though I had had a personality change and was deep in the darkness of my despair. It was not easy to be around me.

When the tranquilizer tablets settled me down and my emotions were under control, about a week later, I had to get back to work to bury myself in something. Otherwise, I would go mad with grief. Work was the only place to hide right now. I just had to go back, to save my sanity.

Chapter Sixteen

There IS a God

I phoned my boss who was understanding, so I went back to work. I worked hard and stayed late at work just to keep myself occupied as I was hurting inside from the pain of losing Angela. Steve was good about it, but I could not focus on the relationship with him. My mind was elsewhere dealing with the crushing sadness inside me.

Three months went by and still nothing. I was just about to give up on ever finding her. Then I got a call one night from the solicitor.

"They have found Trevor and served the papers on him, so he has to appear in court tomorrow. Unfortunately, the custody of your daughter cannot be sorted out tomorrow. His appearance in court is just a formality to set a date for a custody hearing and the court cannot do anything to get your daughter back at this time. You will have to wait for the custody hearing, but I will let you know when that is. I am sorry I can't tell you anything more at

LOSS OF FAITH

this time, but at least things will start to move now," he said.

"Thank you for letting me know," I replied.

A glimmer of hope but my heart is so sad and in so much pain. I miss my daughter so much.

I had lost my faith in everything, God, life, the legal system. There was nothing there to help me. All I could feel was the pain. I was carrying on with life, but like a robot. My spark had gone and part of me was missing.

One thing I cannot understand: if God loves me why would He do this to me? This is more than anyone can bear. I am in my early twenties and have not done anything to hurt anyone, so why me? Why do I have to go through this at such an early age?

My heart and intentions were pure. I only wanted happiness for me and Angela, but happiness seemed to elude me at every turn. Happiness came for a passing moment and then, it was gone. Nobody could do anything for me right now, not my mother, my father, or Steve. I had become an introvert and just buried my pain in my work. That's all I could do to cope. I hated God, religion and anything to do with spiritual beings. It's all a load of rubbish. Nothing had any meaning any more. If Spirit tried to connect with me, I would put up a brick wall and push it all away. There was no way that I was ever going to connect myself to anything that could hurt me in this way. My faith in things had truly gone. My feelings had been locked up and the key thrown away.

If this is what life is all about, I don't want to be part of it anymore. I am better off on my own. That way, I can't get hurt.

I had moved back home with my parents because it was not fair for Steve while all of this was happening. He just didn't know what to do for me. Even though he had become very fond of Angela and missed her, he didn't have any children of his own, and could not understand what I was going through. It's funny how we push people away when we're in so much pain. I felt that I was on self-destruct, trying to hurt myself more by isolating myself from the people I loved.

The solicitor phoned again to say that the custody hearing date had been set and that we needed to prepare for it. It was a month away and that seemed like a lifetime.

I spent time with the solicitor going through everything before the hearing. I dare not ask him what my chances were of getting my daughter back because I was afraid he would say that my chances were slim. I felt powerless, lost and stuck in this moment of not being able to do anything.

At work, I had control over everything, but in my personal life, I had lost hope that things would ever change. I never thought anything could be so painful and destructive.

How could anyone do this to another human being —take something that was not theirs because they did not have a daughter? Trevor's parents wanted mine at all costs. But, Trevor just wanted revenge.

How can this be when I have done them no harm.

I felt sorry for Steve for coming into my life at this difficult time. I just had nothing left to give to him or anyone else. My only focus was to work, hide my pain, and get my daughter back.

The day of the custody hearing arrived. My stomach was in knots and my body felt like a bowl of jelly. I could not smile for anyone. I was so worried that everything would go wrong.

Father had the day off work to go with me for support. While he drove the car, not a single word passed between us. When we entered the court house, the solicitor was waiting and took us to meet the barrister who was scheduled to defend me. We had a long chat and he told me not to worry. It was difficult not to worry as my daughter was so precious to me.

We were in court for two hours. First, they heard my side and then my husband's side. Trevor's parents were with him, smirking at me, as if to say "You will lose." I could hardly stand being there. The judge summed up at the end and gave us his decision. I could not stand to listen as everything was a blur in slow motion. I could see his lips moving but could not hear anything. I was there, but not there. Then the solicitor grabbed one arm, and my father grabbed the other, and they were so excited.

"You've got your daughter back, Patricia—did you not hear the judge?' he asked.

"What?" I replied in a daze.

"You've got Angela back. They have to hand her over tomorrow, so I will go with you," he said, with excitement in his voice.

"I've got her back!" I stuttered in shock.

I grabbed hold of my father and could not let go. The tears and emotion from what had just happened was too overwhelming. I could not move. My body was in collapse mode.

"We will have to leave the court room now," the solicitor said.

LOSS OF FAITH

"Come on, Patricia, let's go," Father said, as he helped me up and walked me out of the court room. When we got outside, we thanked the solicitor for all of his help and headed for home.

"I have to get everything ready for Angela's coming home," I said.

"Don't worry about that. We can do it together. We will go home and relax for a while," he said.

When we arrived home, Father explained to Mother what had happened. She never said a word.

"Make a cup of tea for us all, Ada," Father said.

Mother came back with tea and we sat staring into the fire, not saying a word.

Chapter Seventeen

Killing Me Softly

After tea, we got everything sorted out for Angela coming home. There was a real sense of excitement and I could not wait for her to return. Mother did not say anything. She just huffed and puffed under her breath. Father was excited and determined that this moment would not get spoiled for me. I had arranged for two weeks off from work, so I could spend quality time with her to make sure she felt safe, secure and loved.

After all this time my daughter is coming home.

I just wanted to make sure everything was okay and that nothing could go wrong.

My mother and father had booked two weeks holiday at Blackpool seaside resort and, once Angela was home, and settled for a day, they were going to set off. That meant Angela and I would be on our own for two whole weeks. Father just wanted to make sure we were both okay before they left on holiday. He had definitely

LOSS OF FAITH

planned it so we could have some time on our own with no interference.

I had reconnected with Steve and he was taking some time off work also to take us both out. My heart was pounding with excitement but, part of me was scared that something would go wrong, or that Trevor would skip the country with Angela.

All these thoughts were racing through my head, but all I wanted, was Angela back in my arms.

I went to bed early but could not sleep. My stomach was in knots just thinking about getting her back. I had waited so long for this moment that I could hardly believe it.

I have lost my faith and trust—is this a time to renew it?

I had not yet reunited with Angela. It was too early to say "thank you" because right now, she was not back in my arms.

I tossed and turned all night watching the moonlight through the curtains. My mind was racing with what-if's, my stomach twisted into knots. I got about two hours sleep and woke up to the sound of birds singing in the daybreak. It was a wonderful and happy sound. Today is the day!

I jumped out of bed with a real sense of belief and excitement. I will have Angela back by 10 a.m. today.

I quickly got dressed and ran downstairs to get my breakfast.

"I will go with you to pick up Angela and make sure that nothing goes wrong," Father said.

"Thanks Father, I'll need you there," I replied.

After breakfast, we got into the car and left for the

shop. My stomach was churning with excitement but I could not talk, so we drove in silence.

We arrived at Trevor's mother's shop, got out of the car and headed for the door. My heart was pounding like a drum. As we got closer, Trevor's mother and father opened the door.

"She's all ready to go with you," Trevor's father said.

"Thanks," I replied.

"Come on Angela, you have to go with your mother now," Trevor's mother said. A little face peered around the back of her legs.

"Come on Angela we are going home," I said, bending down and holding my arms out to pick her up.

As soon as I lifted her, she started screaming and crying.

"I don't want to go. I want to stay with my Grandmother and GrandFather," she cried.

"It's all right Angela, your GrandFather is here and you can see your Grandma at home," I replied with a worried voice.

"I don't want to go, I don't want to go!" she kept screaming.

My heart sank and I turned and looked at Trevor's parents who were grinning from ear to ear.

My father looked at me and quickly said, "Come on, take Angela to the car and I will bring her things."

I was in a daze walking to the car because Angela was screaming, "I hate you. I don't want to go."

Tears were streaming down my face. I loved my daughter and wanted her to be happy. I thought she would have missed me but, instead, she hated me.

LOSS OF FAITH

Father quickly loaded the car and we left with Angela still screaming and crying.

"Don't worry. She will settle down," he said, trying to comfort me.

"I hope so, Father. I have never seen her like this," I replied. Nothing I could do or say would comfort her. She screamed and cried all the way home.

When we arrived home, Mother came rushing to the door. "What is all that noise?" she asked.

"Be quiet, Ada. Angela's upset that's all. She's had a traumatic time this morning being up rooted from her grandparents," Father snapped.

We went into the house and Father brought in Angela's things, while Mother made a pot of tea. Angela was still sobbing. I tried to play with her to make her feel at home.

Flashes kept coming back to me of Trevor's parents grinning at the door as Angela screamed her head off. I kept wondering what it was all about.

"We'll have this cup of tea and then your father and I will start packing our suitcases," Mother said.

"Okay, Mother. I know you have things to do since you're going away. I will take Angela for a walk when we've had a drink of tea," I replied.

After the tea, even though Angela was still crying, we got ready and went to visit Susan. I was worried because Angela was so unhappy, and I thought maybe Susan's kids would help cheer her up.

We arrived at Susan's and her kids were in the garden, playing on the swing and slide, having a great time. Angela watched them but would not go to play with them.

LOSS OF FAITH

"What's wrong with her?" Susan asked.

"I don't know. She has been like this since I picked her up this morning," I replied.

Susan tried to play with Angela but she started screaming and crying again, saying she wanted to go back to her grandmother's in Barnsley and that she hated me.

"This is not normal," Susan said.

"I know, but I am hoping she will settle down," I replied.

When Angela wasn't screaming, she was silent and not saying a word.

"I am really worried about her," I said as I burst into tears. "I just don't know what to do for her," I cried.

Susan got up and put her arms around me, saying, "I'm sure she will settle down. It's only been a few hours."

"I know, but when we were leaving, Trevor's mother and father were grinning, so something is not right, I just know it," I said, wiping away my tears.

"I'm sure it will all work out," she replied.

We had tea, biscuits and a chat while Angela just sat and said nothing. We tried everything to get her to play with us and Susan's kids, but she would have none of it.

"I'd better go and get Angela to bed," I said. "My parents are going away tomorrow morning and they will want to get to bed early tonight," I said, standing up, putting her coat on. She was limp and floppy, just like a rag doll. That made putting her coat on very difficult.

"Are we going to Grandma's and GrandFather's in Barnsley now?" Angela asked.

"No. We are going to Grandma's and GrandFather's here," I replied.

LOSS OF FAITH

Well, that set her off big time. She stamped her feet and screamed, "No, I want to go to Barnsley. I hate you," she said, and repeated it over and over again.

"This is not normal," Susan said. "I hope they have not done anything to her."

"I hope not, too. I'd better go and get her home." I replied.

Angela cried and screamed all the way home. Everyone looked at me as though I had done something to her. When we arrived home, she was still screaming.

"What on earth is wrong?" Mother asked.

"I don't know. She's been like that all day. She wants to go to Barnsley and she says she hates me. I have tried everything, but nothing I do will help her settle down. She either screams or doesn't say anything. When she's quiet, she's like a limp doll," I replied.

"Give her a day or two. I'm sure she will be all right. Oh, and by the way, we are leaving tomorrow morning at 9 a.m.," Mother replied.

"Okay. I'm going to give Angela some food, bath her and put her to bed. I will stay with her until she falls asleep," I said.

After finishing with her bath, Angela and I got into bed. She was quiet now, not saying a word and just staring at the wall.

I tried talking to her, but there was no response. I tried cuddling her, but she pulled away. This was my daughter and I just didn't know what I could do for her. I felt so helpless.

As she dropped off to sleep, the tears streamed down my face. I wanted this day to be so happy for both of us.

LOSS OF FAITH

What have I done wrong?
"Nothing," a voice said.
I took no notice of the voice as my heart was in so much pain. I just cried, the tears flooding out like the ocean until there were no more tears to shed and I fell asleep.

※ ☆ ※

Chapter Eighteen

Lies & Deception

※ ☆ ※

I suddenly woke up hearing movement and noise upstairs. I looked at the clock. It was 6:00 a.m., and Mother and Father were getting ready to go off on their holiday to *Blackpool*. I stayed in bed until Angela woke up. The first words she spoke were, "I want to go see my Grandma and Granddad in Barnsley."

"We can't just yet," I said.

Then the tantrums started again. "I want to. I want to," she cried.

"Come on, Angela, we will get up and have breakfast," I said.

She threw such a tantrum screaming and shouting, "I hate you, I hate you. I want my Grandma and Granddad." My parents came rushing into the bedroom.

"What's wrong?" Mother shouted.

"I don't know. She wants to go to Barnsley. I told her that we couldn't go and to get up for breakfast, and then,

LOSS OF FAITH

this happened. I just don't know what to do," I cried, tears streaming down my face like a river. I was so lost and did not know what to do for her. It was my worst nightmare.

"Come on Angela, come with me," Father said, as he picked her up off the bed and took her downstairs.

"We don't need this. She'd better calm down by the time we come back from holiday," Mother snapped as she walked out the door.

What am I going to do?

"You will know in eight days," a voice said.

"Why will I know in eight days?" I asked.

"You wait and see," the voice said.

"What?" I asked.

There was silence.

I washed, changed clothes and went downstairs. Father had tried to give Angela her breakfast but she wouldn't eat. I took over but still, no joy.

"I am worried about her, Father," I said.

"I know, but hopefully it's just a problem with her settling down. So let's wait and see what happens. We will be back in ten days, so just keep calm," he replied.

Angela sat there and said nothing. She looked so sad and all I wanted was for her to be happy.

Mother was true to her word and at 9:00 a.m. she and Father set off for *Blackpool*, one of their favourite holiday places.

I started to tidy up the house and get Angela to join in but she would not move.

"Come on Angela, help Mummy," I said.

There was no answer. She just sat in the chair twirling her hair with her finger, sucking her thumb and staring

LOSS OF FAITH

into space, not saying a thing.

"Come on Angela, let's draw some pictures," I said, as I put the paper and pencils out on the floor.

She just looked at me with a disgusting look and said, "No, I hate you."

I got up and walked quickly to the kitchen to dry my tears.

What can I do?

I was beside myself with worry. I tried to take her out into the garden to play on the swing we had. She wouldn't swing. We went back into the house and I tried to play with her toys. She wouldn't play. She kept pushing me away and getting back up on the settee to sit by herself, twirling her hair. I went and sat beside her, not knowing what else to do. We sat there in silence for about an hour. Then I decided I'd try to cook something for lunch.

I cooked her favourite food: fish fingers, chips and beans. She would not eat or drink a thing.

"Come on, Angela, eat your dinner," I said.

"No. I want to go home to Grandma's and Granddad's," she said in a tone of voice I had never heard before. It was demanding.

"We can't go see them just yet. You have just come back home," I replied, looking at her.

"I don't want you! I want my grandma and grandFather! I hate you!" she screamed, tears flowing down her little cheeks.

I just did not know what to say anymore. Nothing I did or said made any difference.

I was really worried now. I cleared the table and washed the pots while Angela sat in silence.

"After lunch, we will go to Susan's house."

"Come on Angela we are going out to see Susan and her kids," I said, getting her coat.

"I don't want to go!" she replied in a real temper, slamming her hand on the table.

This was not my daughter before she lived with them.

"We are going out now, Angela," I replied calmly.

The shouting started again. "I hate you!" she said kicking and screaming as I put her coat on to go out. She screamed and cried all the way to Susan's. Everyone was staring but there was nothing I could do. I just tried to not let it get to me. I was relieved when I get to Susan's.

"I could hear you coming from down the street," Susan said as we walked through her back door.

"I know but she won't stop and I don't know what to do anymore," I said, as tears rolled down my cheeks.

"Come on, Angela, sit down at the table with us and have something to eat," Susan said.

Angela got up at the table but would not touch a thing. She just sat, staring.

Susan kept trying to encourage Angela to eat, but still nothing. I just watched and hoped that she'd settle down and eat. But nothing changed. I was really getting more concerned about her.

"I'm going to take Angela to the doctor because she cannot continue like this. Will you come with me Susan?" I asked.

"Of course I will," she replied.

I used Susan's phone and scheduled an appointment with the doctor an hour later.

When we arrived at his office, he was very nice. I explained everything to him and then, he started talking to Angela.

"Now, Angela, what is the matter?" he asked.

"I want to be with my Grandma and Granddad. They said my mother hated me and they loved me, so I want to be with them," she cried.

"That's not true Angela," he replied.

"Yes it is, and my mummy left me. She did not want me and went off with another man and did not treat me nice. So I hate her!" she screamed.

"Okay, Angela, but why are you not eating?" he asked.

"Because Grandma said if I didn't eat, I would be able to come home," she said, calming down.

The doctor poured a glass of water and handed it to Angela saying, "Have a drink of water, Angela."

She picked up the glass and had a little drink.

I was amazed at what she told him. My mouth was wide open with shock and my heart raced in pain. I burst into tears.

Over the six months that Trevor's parents had kept her, they told her that I was a bad person who had abandoned her, gone off with another man, treated her badly and mistreated her. They told her that they were the only ones who loved her. They had told her so many lies.

She was only four years old.

How anyone could do this to a child, the one person I loved so much, was unthinkable. I was speechless and horrified.

"Come on, Patricia. Just hold it together for Angela. I know it was wrong and hurtful for you both," Susan said.

LOSS OF FAITH

"Have you told her you love her?" the doctor asked.

"I tell her that all the time. I've tried to hold her and cuddle with her but she won't have anything to do with me. What am I going to do? This is the most she has said since I got her back," I replied.

"Well, I can give her something to calm her down for a short time. You will have to bring her in every day so we can give her fluids, and we'll see if she settles down," he said.

"I will do whatever it takes. I just want Angela to be well and happy," I replied.

The doctor called the nurse and she took Angela away to give her fluids, while the doctor wrote out a prescription for medication.

We went to get the medication and then back to Susan's home in silence. Not a word was spoken but the feelings and emotions within me were rising.

"What are you going to do, Patricia?" Susan asked.

"I don't know, other than give her the medication and take her to the doctor's every day. I'll give her lots of TLC and see if it changes with time," I replied.

"I am so angry with Trevor's parents, but I don't want to talk about it in front of Angela," I said.

We stayed at Susan's another hour and then left for home.

I had given Angela one of the tablets. She was a bit calmer, but still would not speak to me.

When we got home, I tried to give her food but she would not eat, so I bathed her and got her ready for bed.

She was like a doll—only moving when I moved her. I put her to bed and sang nursery rhymes to her, trying to

LOSS OF FAITH

get her to remember what we used to do together, but that brought no response. I got into bed and cuddled with her but she did not hug me back. She was like a rag doll and no words were spoken.

"I love you, Angela," I said, hoping that something would stay with her and bring back the good memories.

❋ ★ ❋

Chapter Nineteen

Fateful Decision

    A couple of days passed and Angela was rapidly losing weight. Her eyes were glazed over as she stared into space. I was really worried about her and asked to see the doctor again.

    He was concerned about her also. "If she does not pick up in the next couple of days Patricia, we will have to hospitalize her," he said.

    I burst into tears unable to speak. My head was in a spin.

    What can I do?

    "Bring her back in a couple of days," he said.

    I left not able to speak, I was so upset. I watched her become so weak and thin. I could not eat or sleep myself as I just kept looking at her and watching her breathe.

    My thoughts were all over the place.

    Should I let her go back to her grandparents? Should I let her go into the hospital?

LOSS OF FAITH

I had no one to talk to and no one could make my decision for me. I just wanted my daughter alive and well. I loved her so much and it caused me great anxiety to see her like this. I believed she would literally die if I didn't do something.

I got up the next day and decided to go and see my solicitor and have a talk with him. I phoned his secretary and made an appointment for early afternoon.

When I got there with Angela, he was shocked to see her in her weakened condition. I explained everything to him.

"What do you want to do, Patricia?" he asked.

"I just want my daughter back to her normal self—alive and happy," I replied.

"So, what are you going to do?" he enquired.

I sat there in silence for a very long time and the solicitor just looked at me.

This was the hardest decision I ever had to make. I loved Angela so much. My heart was racing and my thoughts were all over the place. Suddenly, I blurted out, "I cannot let my daughter die," I said, bursting into tears. "Give custody of Angela to her father and I will give up access to see her. I want her to be happy. She hates me and wants nothing to do with me. It will hurt me deeply to give her up and not see her, but what can I do?"

"She is a child and they are evil people. She cannot have a life like this. Just look at her. She is so depressed. I just want her to live and be happy. So that is my decision," I said, as I sobbed and stumbled over my words. I could feel the pain in my heart getting stronger.

"Okay, Patricia. I will draw up the paperwork for you

to sign and I will contact their solicitor. We will plan for them to pick her up in two days. So come in at 2 p.m. tomorrow to sign the papers. You know, Patricia, you are a very brave lady to do this for your daughter and I respect you for putting her first," he said.

"It is breaking my heart to do this, but I have no other choice," I cried.

We left and went straight to Susan's house. I had to tell someone.

Susan saw that I was distraught and made a cup of tea.

"What's wrong Patricia?" she asked.

"I've been to see my solicitor and made my decision about Angela," I said, as I wiped tears from my eyes.

"What decision?" she asked.

"I am giving her up and giving custody to Trevor. I'm giving up my right to see her so she can be happy. I just cannot bear to see her like this, and if I don't do something, she will die. The doctor wants to hospitalize her because he is very concerned. If she has to grow up without me to be healthy and happy, then that's the sacrifice I'm prepared to make. It's going to kill me not to see her, I love her so much. But what choice do I have? It has been a traumatic decision to make, but just look at her," I cried.

Susan threw her arms around me and just held me without saying a word, as I sobbed my heart out.

"I know it was not an easy decision for you but it was the right one. You are very brave to put your daughter first. I respect you for that. When does she leave?" she asked.

"In two days. I will talk to Angela tonight and hope

LOSS OF FAITH

it will make a difference. I need to see her change into herself again. But, I had better go home and get things done," I replied.

I walked home with Angela in a pushchair. She was so weak, she couldn't stand up. I was in a daze. I walked, but could not see anything or anyone. All I could think about was losing my daughter.

When we got home, I tried to feed Angela but she would not have it, so I bathed her and got into bed, singing nursery rhymes to her to help her remember what we used to have.

I decided to tell her what I was going to do, and how much I loved her.

"You are going home to your father and grandparents in two days. I love you and will miss you very much. I just want you to be well and happy," I said, tears streaming down my face.

"I am happy now, Mummy," she said with a smile on her face.

I fell asleep holding her in my arms. I asked God to help me and, if need be, to take my life, not hers.

The next day I woke up feeling movement in the bed. There was Angela, sitting up in bed, as large as life. I have my daughter back—it's a miracle!

"You had to make a great sacrifice. You have done that and now, your daughter will live. Remember you were told you would know what to do in eight days," a voice said.

"Why do you keep doing this to me?" I asked.

There was no answer.

I quickly turned and grabbed Angela and held her so

LOSS OF FAITH

tight. I was so happy just to have her back.

When we got up, she ate and drank and played in the garden until it was time to go to the solicitor's to sign the paperwork.

When we arrived at his office, he could not believe the change in my daughter. She was talkative, moving around, laughing and happy.

"She looks normal. Are you sure you want to let her go?" he asked.

"Yes, she is only normal because I am letting her go," I replied.

"Okay, if that's what you want. Here is the paperwork for you to sign. Trevor's parents will pick her up at 10 a.m. tomorrow from your house," he said.

I gathered up the paperwork and slowly read through it.

After finishing, I placed the papers on the solicitor's desk and picked up the pen to sign. I kept staring at the forms feeling so much pain in my heart. I knew if I signed, that I would never see Angela again until she was old enough to come and find me.

What I am doing? I know this is right for her but I'm going to carry this pain forever. She is the love of my life and I will never be the same without her.

I took a deep breath and quickly signed the forms. So much pain moved through my body that I fainted. When I came around, four people were standing over me. My vision was a blur and I could just barely see the outline of people and heard voices in the distance. Slowly everything came into focus.

"Are you all right?" the solicitor asked.

LOSS OF FAITH

"Yes, thank you," I replied.

On the outside, I seemed okay, but on the inside, I was totally numb.

Chapter Twenty

Merlin to the Rescue

"One of my staff will take you home," I heard my solicitor say with an insistent voice.

"I will take her home," Mary, the office manager quickly said. The office staff helped me and Angela into Mary's car and we started the journey home. I was holding onto Angela and staring out of the window. Everything was moving in slow motion. No one spoke a word.

When we arrived, Mary walked us to the house, unlocked the door with my key and walked inside. She made a cup of tea and just sat there, saying nothing.

This is my last day with Angela. I have to pull myself together and get the most out of the time that we have left together.

"It's all right to go now. I'm fine," I said to Mary.

"Are you sure?" she asked.

"I'm sure. I will be fine. Thank you for bringing us home," I said.

"You are welcome and good luck. You have so much

strength and I admire what you are doing for Angela," she said as she got up and left the house.

This is not going to be easy.

"You are going back to live with your dad, grandma and granddad," I said looking at Angela.

"When, when am I going?" she said, full of excitement and with a beaming smile.

The hurt I felt inside was just ripping me apart. It was like a knife going straight through my heart.

Angela is so happy she is going back. She suddenly has become so happy.

"Tomorrow morning. This is our last day together," I replied trying to hold the tears back.

" Good. Can we pack?" she asked jumping up.

She was just so different.

What have they done to my daughter?

I was so determined to make this day a happy one for her, even though I hurt so much that I just wanted to die.

"Come on, Angela. Let's get changed and then we can play," I said as we walked upstairs to get sorted out.

I got Angela changed and we came downstairs. I spent the rest of the day singing songs, playing with her, making her laugh, cuddling with her and giving her so much love. I wanted her to remember this day and what we had together. I just hoped that something would stay in her memory and maybe one day, it would surface to bring her back to me. Then, we could talk and make up for what we had missed. I only wanted the best for her and her happiness. Those were my hopes, dreams and wishes.

Would that happen with Trevor's parents? I can only hope so and have faith in the future.

LOSS OF FAITH

Angela was such a different person now that she was going back. We laughed, she ate her dinner and was so talkative.

This is what I wanted—a happy child. I know now what I am doing is for the best for her. No matter how I feel.

That night, I packed all of Angela's things except what she needed in the morning. I bathed her, got into bed with her and sang nursery rhymes, but with a heavy heart. I knew that this would be the last time I would spend the night with her. I held her so tight. I just didn't want to let her go. She fell asleep. *Am I doing the right thing for her happiness? I hope that it is. I know my choice is for her and not for myself. Angela, I love you so much.*

I cried myself to sleep. I felt so alone and helpless.

I had remembered to set the alarm because I wanted to spend some time with Angela before she left. Everything was ready. I bathed and fed her early so we could go for a walk and have some play time. We walked to the play ground and she got on the swings and slides. She was laughing and playing. I put on a smile, but inside, I was eaten up with the pain of losing her. She was so excited at going back to her dad and grandparents. What I was doing was out of my love for her so she could be happy.

I looked at my watch and it was 9:30 a.m.

"Come on Angela. Let's go and meet your grandma and granddad from Barnsley. They will be here soon," I said.

We got home and I sat her on my knee. "I love you so much, Angela," I said as I held her tight.

Right at that very moment there was a knock at the door and my heart sank.

LOSS OF FAITH

"It's your grandma and granddad, Angela. They've come for you," I said.

Her face lit up and she jumped off my knee and ran to the door with excitement.

I opened the door and there they were, with those smirking grins on their faces.

"Come on, Angela, let's go home," her granddad said.

I was in so much distress I could not speak. Like a robot, I carried things to the car to be loaded. I knew if I said anything, that I would burst into tears, and I was not about to let them see that happen.

I picked up Angela, kissed her and whispered in her ear, "I love you," and handed her over to her grandma who was sitting in the car.

When the car started to move, Angela waved from the back seat. My heart fell into a million pieces. The entire scene was in slow motion. I watched the car move out of sight and ran into the house sobbing my heart out.

I just did not want to live without my daughter. I picked up a carving knife and stood there looking at it, as I turned the blade towards my chest with both of my hands on the handle. I pushed the knife with force towards my chest. At that point, some invisible being, grabbed my hands and stopped me. The knife was only two inches away from my chest. The being had such great strength that I could not fight it. I fell, dropping the knife. I sobbed so hard, lying there on the floor, that I cried myself to sleep.

I woke up two hours later and found myself on the settee in the living room with a blanket thrown over me. I didn't remember getting up.

How did that happen?

LOSS OF FAITH

I remembered something pulling the knife away from my chest and then, me dropping to the floor in distress.

Someone looked after me, but who?

"It's not your time to go. You have many years ahead of you," a voice said.

"Merlin is that you?" I asked.

"Yes, Patricia. It is," he answered.

"You looked after me," I said.

"Yes, Patricia. I felt your pain and now, I have to go," he said.

"Why do I have to keep going through all this Merlin? I am twenty-two years old and so much has happened in my life. There's been so much pain. Why can't it change Merlin?" I asked.

"We all have our journey, Patricia, and everything gets revealed in its own good time. You are learning for things to come. Be patient," he said, as his voice disappeared into thin air.

I was so alone. My parents would not be back for two days. I felt so much pain inside as I missed Angela so much. I hoped and prayed that she was happy and well.

I had to keep myself busy for the next couple of days just to deal with my loss. I cleaned the house and visited with friends. I came back to the house late as I did not want to spend time on my own thinking too much. When I did, I could not stop crying. Angela was always in my thoughts, and losing her was driving me to despair.

The night before my parents came home I felt worried.

What will they say?

Mother was never understanding of me and my actions, but hopefully, Father would be supportive. I expect-

LOSS OF FAITH

ed grief from my mother, but I was in no way ready to take it. My emotions were very unstable.

I still cannot understand why all these things keep happening to me and why my life will not change for the better.

As I had these thoughts, a circle of white light appeared in my bedroom and swirled around. I watched it go round and round in a circle. There was warmth exuding from the light and I felt it pulling me towards it. Suddenly, I was up in the air, looking down, floating and being pulled into the light. I felt very calm inside, almost like dream state. There was a presence in the room and I could feel it moving around.

"Who are you?" I asked.

"I am Matthew, from Atlantis," he answered.

"Why don't you show yourself, Matthew?" I asked.

With that, a male figure appeared, dressed all in white. He was a humble looking man who appeared to be in his fifties.

"I am here to help and support you through this traumatic time, Patricia. I'm here to help heal your heart and learn the lessons you need to learn for your soul to grow," he said.

"But, I have so much pain from the loss of my daughter. How could I have faith in God right now? He has deserted me and left me with nothing. The only thing I had and loved, was Angela," I cried.

"We will talk again," Matthew said.

I could feel myself being lowered to my bed as the white, swirling light faded away.

I lay in bed feeling numb inside and slowly dropped off to sleep.

Chapter Twenty-One

Letting Go, Confessions & TLC

I woke up early the next day knowing that my parents would be back about noon. I had to make sure the house was spick and span so Mother would not complain so much. She always had something to say even if the house was perfect. So I had my breakfast and then set to hoovering and dusting the house, cleaning the bathroom and toilet, making sure everything was back in its original state, before they got home. I had let the house go with what had been happening with Angela and my emotions, even though Mother was fanatical about a clean and tidy house.

I decided to cook them a meal for when they got home. They would be tired and I was not in the mood to go to the fish and chip shop and face people. I had bought stew meat and decided to make stew and dumplings as that would slowly cook and wouldn't burn. I chopped up the vegetables and placed them with the meat and seasoning to cook in the stew pan.

At 12:30 p.m. I heard the sound of Father's car pulling onto the driveway and my heart dropped.

This is going to be interesting. I dread facing Mother—I know she will not understand.

My mother was heavy-footed so I could hear her stomping down the driveway in her leather soled shoes. My heart pounded with anxiety. She pushed the door open and dropped her handbag on the table. Her eyes were everywhere looking at the state of the house. Anyone would think I was a raving teenager who would wreck the joint. Father was unpacking the car, ferrying bags and suitcases to the house. My mother always took a lot of clothes on holiday. I felt sorry for him.

My mother wandered around the house looking in every corner. It felt like I was in prison with the warden checking everything out. She suddenly came back into the kitchen.

"Where is Angela?" Mother asked in an argumentative tone, almost like she was looking for a fight.

"I will explain later, after you've eaten," I replied, turning to set the table and put out the dinner. I was trying to avoid confrontation as I wasn't ready for that. I knew it would happen but I didn't want it just yet. My heart was beating fast and my eyes filled with tears. I desperately was trying to hold them back, as I hated to cry in front of Mother.

"What have you been up to?" she snapped, pulling my arm so I would look at her.

"Nothing! Will you just leave me alone and have your dinner?" I snapped back, pulling my arm away from her. I

LOSS OF FAITH

just wish she would sit and eat and leave me alone.

Father walked in and said, "What is going on?"

"She won't tell me where Angela is," Mother said, angrily.

"Where is she, Patricia?" Father asked.

"Have some food and I will tell you then," I replied, with my stomach churning round and round in knots. It was making me feel sick.

"Okay, Ada, give the girl a break and let's eat what she has prepared," he said, giving me a knowing look.

I put dinner out and they both ate. I could not eat with them and had not eaten anything for the last couple of days. So I just sat at the table trying to gather my thoughts as to what to say. No one spoke a word while eating. Mother kept staring at me—really mad—and Father kept looking up at me with a great deal of love in his eyes.

After they had finished eating, I cleared the table and washed the pots. Mother sat there with her arms folded. She gave me that look that she usually gives to say, "I am not moving until I know what is going on." Father had a cigarette. I knew that he could feel my pain. I tried not to look at her but I felt her eyes burning into my back.

My heart was in my mouth as I turned from washing up to look at the table and see my mother's face. If looks could have killed, I would have been dead.

I quickly said, "I'm not talking to you in here. You will have to come into the living room." I rushed out of the kitchen with my stomach all tight and tangled and sat in the arm chair which I knew would be next to my father—my security blanket.

LOSS OF FAITH

Father calmly walked into the room, sat in his usual chair, and Mother followed behind, stomping her feet with her arms folded across her chest. As she entered the living room, she said, "Well, my lady, are you going to tell us what has gone on? I know it is something bad as nothing is straight forward with you. We've only been away ten days and something has gone wrong, I can feel it," she moaned in her groany, snappy voice.

"Do you always have to be like this with me? Can't you just give me support right now? You are always so mean to me," I said, bursting into tears. I was so angry with myself for crying.

"Ada, sit down and let her talk," Father said with anger.

"Oh, take her side," Mother said.

"Just sit down and shut up," Father snapped.

Mother muttered under her breath as she dropped into her chair with a thud. Shuffling about until she got comfortable, her face was like thunder. She didn't like it when Father took control.

"If she's going to be like this, I don't want her to be here while I tell you what has happened," I cried, as tears ran like a stream down my face. I could hardly breathe while I was sobbing. My heart felt like someone had put a knife through it.

"Your mother won't say a word, so you can just talk and we will listen," Father said in a sympathetic quiet voice.

I re-lived the pain of what had happened in the last ten days and my heart raced. I felt sick in my stomach, but had to tell the whole story (about Angela, not about my trying to kill myself). Father sat listening and looking at me with his loving soft eyes, while mother kept fidgeting and glaring at me through her glasses.

I sat and never stopped crying, gasping for air in between the sobs, as I told them everything that had happened—Angela's behavior, the doctors, what Angela had told the doctor, the decision I had made, and how upset and helpless I had felt about it all, and how all I wanted was my daughter's happiness. When I had finished and gone quiet, still sobbing my heart out, Mother stood up and in a disgusted tone shouted, "You have done what? You've given up your own child? What kind of mother are you?"

"I knew you wouldn't understand. Can't you see what pain I'm in? Do you think I did this for me? You're the one who's not a good mother. You are so horrible to me," I screamed as the anger flew through my body and my fists clenched.

I could have put my hands around her throat and squeezed all the life out of her. I shouldn't be thinking like this, all I have ever wanted was my mother to understand me and love me.

Just at that moment my father leaned over, and touched my clenched fist. It was like an angel had touched me with love.

"Go and make a cup of tea, Mother. I want to talk to Patricia," Father said. He looked at her as if to say, "Just leave the room—Now!"

Mother was mad and stormed out of the room. Father glanced over at me with those loving eyes and in his soft, caring voice said, "Patricia, no matter what your mother says—and I will deal with her—you have made the right decision for Angela. I know it's painful for you right now, but time is a great healer and I know you will see Angela again. But, you did not tell us everything did you?"

"What do you mean?" I said, with a puzzled look.

"You know what I mean. I think I only need to say that I saw a knife, don't I?" he asked, with so much love in his eyes.

"The loss of Angela gave me so much pain, that I didn't want to carry on," I cried, wiping the tears away.

"Well, I'm glad they did not let it happen, as I would have missed you so much. You are such a sensitive girl and so much has happened to you in your life. I wish you could find some peace and happiness for once. I love you Patricia. You are such a special girl with so much to offer," he said, getting up from his chair.

"Come here, let me give you a cuddle," he said, holding out his arms.

I got up and just dropped into his arms, sobbing my heart out, my tears wetting his shirt. "I miss her so much," I said.

"I know Patricia," he replied.

I felt so much love and strength from my father and knew he was sharing my pain.

Mother brought the tea in, looked at us and snapped, "What is going on?"

"Never you mind, Ada. We will just drink our tea quietly and then Patricia is going to go and lie down on her bed," he said in his stern voice while looking at my mother as if to say, "Enough is enough." He had a way in dealing with her.

That was Father's way of getting me out of the way so

LOSS OF FAITH

he could talk to Mother.

We all sat down and drank our tea in silence. Mother just stared at me and looked at Father with anger. She never liked to be told to shut up. I just stared into the fire, watching the flames dance around with their orange glow, feeling my heart had been ripped out. The emptiness made my body feel like a shell of nothingness. I was numb all over.

As soon as I had finished my tea, I got up, said goodnight and went upstairs so they could talk. Father answered but Mother remained silent. I felt a weight had been lifted off my shoulders. My head hit the pillow and I fell asleep.

I woke up the next morning and could not believe I had slept for about twelve hours. It was about 10 a.m. and I could hear voices. I got up, had a bath, dressed and went downstairs. As I walked into the living room, Mother gave a look of displeasure. Father smiled and asked, "Did you have a good sleep, Patricia?"

"Yes, Father. I can't believe I slept for such a long time," I replied.

"Well, you must have needed it," he said smiling.

I went to the kitchen, made a cup of tea, and came back into the living room to sit with Father. I felt safe with him. He just had this sense of knowing and said the right things at the right time.

"Well, Patricia. I'm going to tell your brother and sister what happened and then, this will not be spoken of again in this house. You have made your decision and it's the right one. I want everyone to know that, and then, no more questions will be asked," he said.

LOSS OF FAITH

"That's all right, Father. I just don't want to be interrogated by everyone or keep getting those black looks that Mother is so good at giving. I just want to get on with my life and deal with my grief in my own way," I replied.

"I know, Patricia. I'm trying to close it down for you so no one asks any questions," he said.

"I know," I replied.

Then there was silence. I just stared into the flames of the fire, drinking my tea and still feeling the pain in my heart from losing Angela, wondering what she was up to, and whether she was happy.

What am I going to do without her? I feel so alone and constantly wonder what she is doing. I hope she's all right and happy.

Angela's happiness was very much in my heart. I couldn't get her out of my thoughts.

All this had created the biggest test of my faith. I had pushed everything away because I felt that no one cared. The one thing I truly loved had been taken away from me. I hated God with such vengeance. This was now my spiritual battle. I was so determined to walk away from everything I had known in my life—God, angels. I did not believe in anything anymore. If there were such things as God or angels, they would not let you go through all of this. So as far as I was concerned, I had been imagining things all my life and really nothing existed. My anger against God was so strong, that I burned my Bible on the fire one night. My life had been a roller coaster ride and this was the last straw. Beings did try to come to me in my dreams and around me but I had totally shut down and never wanted to be part of it again.

LOSS OF FAITH

Father tried to talk to me on many occasions about shutting out God, but I just would not listen. Nothing would change my mind. I remembered what Father had said back in February—that I would get divorced by September and end up with nothing. Even that could not have prepared me for what happened and it certainly did not change my opinion about God.

The pain of losing Angela never went away. Every birthday, Christmas, school open day, and parent evenings, brought more pain and tears. I thought time would heal, but in this case, the pain never subsided.

I just learned to put it in a compartment somewhere deep inside and keep it controlled so everyone would think I was all right when I really wasn't. It is funny how you can fool people because most people look at what is on the outside. They never see what's on the inside—the real you.

Through all of this, the one person I had neglected was Steve. He had been there for me, but I could not talk to him about my feelings and what I was going through. So, I moved home and asked him to leave me alone for a while, which he did.

One night, Father said, "You can't just sit there every night after work and stare at the fire."

"I know, Father, but I find it difficult to be happy without Angela," I replied.

Just at that moment, the phone rang and Father answered it. "Yes, she's here. Just a minute and I'll get her," Father said, beckoning me to the phone.

"Who is it?" I asked.

"It's Steve," he said, handing me the phone.

LOSS OF FAITH

We chatted for a while and I agreed to go out with him on Saturday, which felt good. I needed to get out and do things. Father was right.

"I'm glad you are going out," he said.

"So am I," I replied.

I knew that Father didn't like Steve, but I think he was just happy for me to get on with my life.

On Saturday, Steve came to pick me up. It seemed strange, because the last time Angela had come with us. He felt uneasy about it and I could sense his nervousness and anticipation that I would get upset. I managed to hold everything back and just got in the car.

I could tell he was pleased to see me. He kept talking to make sure I was all right and to fill the conversation so I would not have time to get upset. We drove all the way to Cleethorpes, a seaside town, walked on the beach, had something to eat, and wandered around.

On the way back, Steve asked, "When are you coming back home with me?"

"Tonight or tomorrow, depending on what time we get back to my parents' house," I replied.

He smiled and said, "It will be tonight. I will get you home in time to pick up your things."

We got back to my parent's house about 8:30 p.m. and went into the house. Steve sat down and I made him a cup of tea.

"I am moving in with Steve so I have come to take my things," I said, looking at my father.

"Okay, Patricia, as long as that's what you want," he replied.

"It is," I answered.

LOSS OF FAITH

Mother looked very happy that I was going. It brought a smile to her face.

I quickly got my things together, said goodbye to my parents, gave Father a big hug and headed for Steve's place. We needed time to spend on our own. After my trauma, I just needed some love and happiness in my life and to laugh again. It had been so long since I had laughed.

It was obvious when I got to Steve's place, that he had anticipated my coming back. The lights were on in the house and when I entered the back door, the house was clean and tidy. It was obvious his parents had been down and had prepared the place ready for my homecoming. There were fresh cut flowers in a purple vase on the coffee table and food in the fridge. I got on very well with his parents and they loved both Angela and me. Steve had all the candles around that I had bought and was going around quickly lighting them.

"Trying to be romantic are we?" I asked, laughing. Steve was not a romantic person, so to see him trying to light candles and get just the right piece of music was funny, but the Carpenters' record started to play. I loved the Carpenters. He would much prefer to listen to Led Zepplin, Black Sabbath, or 10CC, so he was making an effort to please me and make me happy. This set me off laughing so much my stomach hurt.

Steve came running over, put his arms around me and said, "I have missed you so much."

"I'm glad you missed me," I replied.

We sat on the settee cuddling each other until 3:00 a.m. just holding each other and listening to music. It felt so good to be held in his arms. It made me feel loved and

LOSS OF FAITH

secure. This is just what I need right now. Although my mind kept wandering and thinking about Angela. I missed her so much. Nothing could replace that love I had for her.

Steve said "Shall we go to bed now?"

"Yes," I replied.

We got up and walked upstairs. When I entered the bedroom all the photos of Steve and me and Angela were still up.

"Thank you for leaving the photos. I need my good memories," I said.

"Didn't know what to do but Mum said to leave them for you to decide, so I did," he replied.

I burst into tears and he just stepped forward and placed his arms around me, holding me tight.

We sat on the bed and I cried myself to sleep in his arms.

Chapter Twenty-Two

Body Collapse

Over the next few months, Steve and I became closer. Through all of this chaos, I had buried myself in my work to hide my pain. Apparently, my efforts paid off as I received a promotion and a large pay raise. However, this just covered up what was really going on inside.

Everyone saw this confident, independent, self-assured, ambitious, highly motivated, and successful person. That was the outward appearance. The inside person was crumbling in unhappiness from not having Angela.

I was trying to be happy. I loved Steve but there was always that little bit of me missing.

We usually went shopping in Doncaster on Saturday and this weekend was no different. We got into town about 10:30 a.m., walked down the high street, and as we crossed the road, I suddenly collapsed.

I could hear cars screeching to a halt and Steve's voice shouting, "Call an ambulance!" I was semi-conscious and

LOSS OF FAITH

could hear what was going off around me, but everything I saw had a mist-like fog around it. My eyes were open but not a great deal was happening.

I heard the ambulance pull up and could see faces as they put me in the vehicle and transported me at high speed to the hospital. Angelic faces were all around me, telling me I was going to be all right. That was the last thing I remembered until I woke up in a private room in a hospital bed. The consultant came to see me and told me I was very lucky. I had a ruptured appendix with no warning signs. He told me I was lucky to be alive. I hated hospitals. All I wanted was to know when I would be going home.

Steve stayed with me most of the time except for going home to bed. I was having panic attacks as I could not stand being in a hospital, so the consultant decided to let me go. As soon as I was home, I was fine. Steve took time off work to check on me and make sure I did not do anything I was not supposed to do. The district nurse came to visit me and took my stitches out. My recovery was good and I was back at work within ten days. All of my spiritual experiences were coming back to me, including my visions. I could not mistake the angelic beings telling me that I was going to be all right. Now, I was fit and well, when just a few days before, I thought I was dying.

Maybe I should pick things up again.

Steve had been very caring through my illness and I appreciated that.

My new life with Steve is just about to begin and I really have to try and make it work and not let my unhappiness over my daughter stop my relationship from working.

LOSS OF FAITH

Over the next few months, I tried very hard to put things behind me. I was still sentimental at birthdays and Christmas, but Steve understood and was very supportive.

After work, we went out a lot, had a good time with friends and laughed a great deal. It helped me to numb the pain inside. At least on the outside I was laughing. I often wondered, though, what my daughter was doing and how she looked now that she was growing up. She was always on my mind and I often wondered whether she thought about me.

I had lived with Steve for just over twelve months and then one evening over dinner, he just said out of the blue, "Would you marry me?" It took me by surprise, my heart raced and I bumbled out, "Yes!"

We both told our parents together. Steve's parents were so happy.

"It's about time," his dad said.

"We love you as a daughter," his mother said. When we saw my parents, Father gave me a cuddle and whispered in my ear, "If it's what you want and it makes you happy, I am happy for you." He turned to Steve and said, "You better look after her or you will have me to answer to," he said, smiling.

Well Mother was Mother, and just sat there forcing a smile but not saying anything as usual. We then went home and started planning our wedding. We didn't want anything fancy, just a registry office marriage, so that's what we did. We invited close family and friends and had a quiet ceremony at Barnsley Registry Office. I bought a simple cream knee length dress and a big brown floppy

LOSS OF FAITH

hat. I loved hats. Angela lived in Monk Bretton in Barnsley and it was so close to the registry office. I wish she could have been there. Straight after the wedding, we left for two weeks in Torquay for our honeymoon. It seemed funny to be married again but it did feel good. The only person missing from my wedding was my daughter and that saddened my heart. This kept going through my mind over and over again.

We were blessed with good weather on our honeymoon and had a really good time as Mr. and Mrs. Everyone was friendly and the hotel had made a special effort with balloons, and a special meal and drinks on arrival. We were not expecting that.

When we got back, we decided we had lived in a pit house for far too long. We wanted to buy a home. After a long search, we found a bungalow that was being built and decided to purchase it. It was exciting to be buying our new home as a married couple.

We were both excited and kept going down to the plot to watch each phase happen. A three bedroom, detached bungalow.

Angela would love this.

Chapter Twenty-Three

Premonition

While our home was being built, I started having bad feelings but could not put my finger on why. I had managed to suppress this sort of thing for a long time, but this feeling would not go away. I started dreaming and my dreams were disturbing. I would see myself walking away from Steve. But, I loved Steve, and nothing would make me do that. So, I just kept pushing things away.

Then one night, we invited friends to our home. I had cooked a meal, we had some wine, and music was playing. We were all laughing, but I could not help feeling that something was about to happen. I tried to push it away but this time, it would not go.

Our friends were staying over as they had done before, so that was nothing new. We all went upstairs to bed. About 3:00 a.m. I went to the bathroom and when I came out, there was my husband, with my girlfriend, in my bed.

I was horrified when she said, "My husband is waiting for you in the next bedroom."

"I don't think so," I said, as I picked up the bed and turned it upside down on top of them. I grabbed my coat, purse, door keys, car keys, and ran down the stairs and out of the back door. I was shaking like a leaf as I threw my things into the car and drove off. I could not go home to my parents so I found a quiet place to park and sat shaking all over, my heart pounding like the beating of a drum. I couldn't stop shaking and crying.

Why would he do this to me?

I was sobbing so hard I could hardly breathe. I kept looking at the stars and asking, "Why me?" My head was fuzzy and so tired it felt as though my head was going to burst. I just cried myself to sleep in the car. I woke up to the sun shining through the windscreen. I had probably snatch an hour's sleep and felt emotionally drained and exhausted. I didn't know what to do, so I decided to try to eat. I drove and found a café to have breakfast and a cup of tea, but my mind was racing with last night's events. The café owner kept looking at me and eventually asked, "Are you okay, Miss?"

"Yes thanks, just got a lot on my mind," I replied.

Maybe I have been wrong by pushing God away, Maybe He is mad with me.

I could not get away from the strong feelings that warned me that something was going to happen. But, I was not ready to accept everything, yet.

I phoned in sick at work and then went home to get washed and changed. I knew Steve would have gone to work and would not be back until the afternoon.

After going home, I went to visit my friend, Susan,

LOSS OF FAITH

and we chatted for a long time. When I looked at my watch it was 6:00 p.m.

I better go home and see what he has to say for himself. I got up and my heart was racing.

What possible excuse could he give that would explain his behavior?

My legs were like jelly as I walked home and my mind raced with thoughts of what had happened the night before.

As I got near the house, I could see the lights on and the curtains drawn. I stood at the gate for about ten minutes before deciding to go in.

I unlocked the door and there was an eerie stillness in the air. You could have heard a pin drop.

I put my bag down, went into the kitchen, made a cup of tea, sat at the table and stared into the fire. I could feel Steve standing in the doorway but I would not look at him. There was silence for about fifteen minutes.

"What have you got to say for yourself?" I asked, turning to look at him.

"I'm sorry. What started as a joke, ended up being something else," he said.

"I did not see it as a joke," I replied.

"I know and I am sorry. I don't want us to split up. I want us to work it out," he said.

"Well, we will just have to see. I am off to bed," I said getting up and walking past him.

I know I am not going to accept 'sorry' and let it pass.

The next month was strained. We went down to see our new house being finished, but all the pleasure and joy of it had gone.

LOSS OF FAITH

We shopped for furniture and curtains and things like two strangers. I just could not get by this. I still had this bad feeling inside me that was questioning who Steve was and what he was really like.

I was married again and things were already going wrong.

Is it me? Am I doing something wrong? Am I too soft? Am I a fool?

I questioned myself so hard that I got to the point of no return.

No, it is not me. I am a loving person. I give all the time but am not getting anything back. I trust so easily and then get let down.

When we were ready to move into our new home, Steve asked, "Can we give things a go in the new house and get back to what we had?"

I had a bad feeling inside, but said, "Yes. Okay."

The only way I was going to find out, was to say "Yes," as then, he would be comfortable, and we would be back to normal. This way, I would find out, but at the same time, not get hurt as I could protect my heart.

The next month went all right. Things appeared to be normal, but there was a great deal of doubt in my mind and that bad feeling just would not go away.

A week later, I was attending a board meeting at work when I became physically sick and had to go home. When I arrived, there were two cars on the driveway. My heart sank. I went into the house and heard loud music and laughter coming from the living room. When I opened the door, there was alcohol everywhere and five people were on my living room floor having what I would describe as

LOSS OF FAITH

a sexual five-sum. All bodies were intertwined with each other. I was so shocked, I screamed. Everyone looked up at me and said, "Come on. Join in." Steve got up to get me, and I ran out of the house, got in my car and set off at high speed. My heart was in my mouth and my emotions were bouncing all over the place. I found a quiet place to stop and sobbed my heart out. I just could not believe what I had seen.

What am I going to do?

"See this through Patricia. It will come to an end," a voice said.

"Oh, go away! I hate you!" I screamed. "How dare you put me through this and expect me to have anything to do with you."

I sat in the car for about three hours before deciding to go home. I certainly could not go to my parents' house. There would be too many questions. So I drove home. By the time I got there, only Steve's car was on the driveway. I parked and just sat in the car for a while.

Why is God putting me through this? Oh, you are so stupid. There is no God to look after you. Everything you've been taught is a load of rubbish.

There was so much pain inside that my life seemed worthless. I had so much to give but never seemed to get anything back, except hurt.

How much more can I take?

I got out of the car and walked into the house. It was as though I had just awakened from a bad dream. When I walked inside, it seemed like I was there, but not there. It felt as though there were two dimensions. There was a great deal of mist and I could see spirits everywhere.

LOSS OF FAITH

Steve walked into the kitchen and shouted, "How dare you show me up in front of my friends? It's your fault. I go and do other things as you are always working at your high end job, mingling with the big boys, while I'm at home. You're useless as a wife," he said.

Suddenly, I felt a great calmness come over me. My mouth opened and I said calmly, "So, you are hiding behind my work. You knew what I did when I met you and nothing has changed. I just watch the money disappear through your drinking and gambling. There is nothing wrong with me and tomorrow, when you are sober, we are going to talk to your parents."

"How did you know about my gambling?" Steve shouted.

"I just did," I replied.

I had no idea, as I knew it was not me talking.

Steve's parents adored me, and it was time for them to know about their son and see if they could help.

I went to bed before things really got out of hand. Steve slept on the settee in the living room.

The next day we both had the day off and went to visit his parents.

They knew something was wrong as I was such a wreck.

"What's wrong Patricia?" his mother asked with a worried look on her face.

I burst into tears and told them the whole story. When I had finished, Steve's dad took him into the living room and his mother made me a cup of tea.

"I am so sorry, Patricia. You work so hard and this should not have happened to you. You are such a special and loving person. I am so sorry my son could do this to you. I hope you can sort it out and forgive him and give it another go," she said.

I always try to sort things out and make things work, but am I not sure this time.

My head was all over the place, flitting from one thing to another and looking at the negatives of our relationship. I could not stop it. I started thinking of my music.

I did some singing in clubs and pubs in the evenings and on weekends. Steve went everywhere with me. He would get jealous about how I looked at the microphone and how I got the attention and not him.

I had recently been offered a recording contract for a major record label and had to make a decision.

When I am doing something I love, why does someone always get in the way?

I wanted my marriage and my singing career to work, but I had a bad feeling about things.

When Steve finished talking to his dad, he looked sheepish.

"I think this will resolve it, Patricia," his dad said. "Steve, what do you have to say to Patricia?"

"I am sorry," Steve said.

I could tell by the look on his face that he did not mean it, but that was no surprise.

We left and headed for home. There was an uncanny silence in the car as we drove. When we arrived at the house, I made a cup of tea and sat in silence in the living room, just mulling things over in my head, before going to bed. I just wanted to sleep and get away from him.

The next couple of days were quiet. Steve didn't say

much and neither did I. We were like two ships passing in the night on a cold winter's day.

Then one night, Steve said, "If this marriage is going to work, you have to give up singing."

"Why should I give up my singing to make the marriage work?" I asked.

"I will stop drinking and gambling, if you give up your singing. That way, we have both changed something. So think about it," he said, walking out of the living room.

Do I want my marriage to work or to sing? I already have one failed marriage and do not want another, but I do want to sing. Why can't life just be simple? Why are there always conditions where I have to be the one to give up the most? When will life change and go in my favour?

I had not told my parents anything that had been happening, and I wanted to talk to my father, as he would give me a straight answer.

On the weekend, I went alone to see my parents.

When Mother went shopping, I told my father what had been happening and what had been said about giving up my singing. I was quite shocked at his answer, "Give up your husband and do your singing. He is not going to change."

"But, I want my marriage to work," I replied.

"Heavy drinkers and gamblers don't change. They only try to change and then they go back to normal as they can't sustain it. So, you have my advice, but only you can make the decision," he said.

I left feeling puzzled. I was sure Father would have wanted me to make my marriage work.

Steve was pushing me for a decision. He was not go-

LOSS OF FAITH

ing out except for my singing. He was not drinking alcohol or having mood swings and we were not arguing, so things seemed to be improving.

I felt pressure from all sides. Steve wanted a decision. The record company wanted a decision.

Why can't I just have both?

❀ ★ ❀

Chapter Twenty-Four

The Power of Decision

Father's words kept running through my head. It was a nightmare. Steve had given me until the weekend to make up my mind. I had to make a decision and hopefully, it would be the right one. I spent all week thinking about it.

Can Steve maintain the change? Will everything be all right? I do not want another failed marriage. But most of all, I really want to sing. My singing is my passion and makes me feel whole and at peace with myself. In fact, it is my whole being. Why do I have to make a choice? Nothing makes sense to me anymore. I have pushed God and my spiritual side away and really have no faith in anything anymore. What is the meaning of my life?

It was a difficult decision that I had to make and it took me back to feeling the pain of losing Angela. My singing had become as important as my daughter and yet, again, I had to make a decision that involved another person. I chose to save my marriage and give up what I truly wanted.

Steve was happy with my decision because he had got what he wanted.

I hated him for that and for cheating on me. My emotions were in turmoil and my heart felt so much pain and unhappiness. I had to try to forget what had happened if I was to make my marriage work, but it was not easy. On the outside, I was smiling, but on the inside, I feared what could happen again. It tore me apart, the thought of him cheating on me, but I still loved him and had to trust him.

I am the one who is doing all the giving up but, I just do not want another failed marriage.

During the next six months, there was a great deal of pain and sadness in my heart, because I had given up my music and my recording contract to try and make my marriage work. Steve appeared to be trying too, so nothing seemed to be wrong.

We went out one Saturday night with about eight friends and everyone was drinking heavily, except me. I liked to be able to see what was happening. There was a great deal of whispering from the men and the women were giggling. I was just bored.

I saw the men get a paper bag and all the car keys were put inside. Then, they asked each woman to pick a set of keys. I was horrified. I stood up, walked all the way home, got undressed and went to bed.

About thirty minutes later, Steve came home drunk and would not stop shouting. He pulled me out of bed and flung me across the room. He kept hitting me and blood was pouring from my nose. There was a cut on my head.

LOSS OF FAITH

The more I tried to escape, the more he hit me. I thought he was going to kill me. All he could say was, "How dare you show me up in front of my friends!"

I didn't say a word.

Then, there was a pause as he had to go to the toilet. As he shut and locked the door, I ran for the phone and dialled the police. I managed to get my name and address out in my distress before Steve came running out of the toilet. He ripped the phone from my hand and started beating me again. I was terrified for my life. Although I could feel the pain, I was scared and numb at the same time. He was like a madman. His face changed to what I could describe as evil and demonic. He was laughing and enjoying what he was doing. It seemed a lifetime before the police arrived. I thought I was going to die. I was in panic. I could see blood everywhere, including on his fists. It was like a horror movie. This can't be happening—what did I do wrong to deserve this—how much more can I take—where are the police? Just at that point the police arrived, pulled him off me, and dragged him outside as he began to fight one of the policemen. It took two policemen to restrain him.

A police woman came over to me and sat me down.

"I have called a doctor for you and we are taking your husband to the police station. I am staying with you to take a statement," she said. I was covered in blood and sobbing my heart out.

"Why did he do this to me?" I asked, sobbing.

"We don't know yet and we need the doctor to take a look at you," the police woman replied.

I felt awful. Every part of me was hurting, blood everywhere. I caught sight of myself in the mirror, my face covered in blood and swollen. I looked like a beast from hell.

By the time the doctor arrived, I had two black eyes, a busted nose, I was bruised all over and my clothes were covered in blood.

He examined me and made arrangements for me to go to the hospital for x-rays, as he felt I had two broken ribs. An ambulance was called and the policewoman went with me.

"Is there anyone I should call for you?" she asked.

"No. It is too embarrassing and my mother would just not understand," I cried.

I wanted to call Father, but didn't want to worry him and cause another eruption between him and my mother. I needed to sort this out myself.

After the x-rays, it was confirmed that I had two broken ribs and a broken nose. The rest were just cuts and bruises. The police woman took me home and I couldn't speak a word as I was in shock at what had happened. My mind was all over the place and I was hurting all over. It was an emotional roller coaster. We arrived at the bungalow and the police woman turned and looked at me.

"They are keeping your husband overnight so, I will come back in the morning to take your statement," she said.

"Okay," I replied getting out of the car.

I was dreading walking into the bungalow. My memories were so clear. I tentatively opened the door and put the light on. It looked like World War II. Blood was splattered everywhere. Pots, pans, chairs and the table lay bro-

LOSS OF FAITH

ken on the kitchen floor. There was a trail of blood that ran through the bungalow on the carpets and bloody handprints on the walls. In the living room, our cream three piece suite was covered in blood, the television lay on the floor smashed into pieces. This was my worst nightmare. I walked into the bedroom and clothes were thrown everywhere and my jewelry box lay on the floor, its contents scattered all over. My perfume bottles were smashed and the bedroom was overwhelming with the smell. I quickly closed the door and decided to sleep in the spare bedroom. That was the only place not damaged or splattered with blood.

Once in bed, I could not stop crying. My mind would not stop working.

Why did this have to happen to me, after giving up my singing? I hate God and everything, I tried to make my marriage work. What I have done wrong?

There was nothing now, just silence in the house and I felt truly alone and desperate.

I started to drop off to sleep when I felt this huge weight on my back. I could not move and could hardly breathe. I was terrified and wanted to scream. My mouth would open but nothing would come out. It felt like someone was trying to rip my soul from my body. Shear panic set in.

Go away and leave me alone!

After about ten seconds, something released me. I jumped up and put the light on, but nothing was there. I left the light on and stayed in bed thinking about what had just happened. I really could not work it out and did not want to fall asleep just in case it came back. So, I watched daylight break with this terrified feeling inside.

Will they let Steve come home? What will happen next?

I felt sick to my stomach.

The policewoman said she would come at 9:00 a.m. so I got up and slowly got ready. She was true to her word and, at that exact time, she knocked at the door.

We sat down in the living room and I went through the evening's events, telling her what had happened as she wrote everything down. At the end, I signed my statement. I just felt numb, exhausted physically and mentally, and my pain was horrific.

"What about Steve? What is going to happen to him?" I asked.

"They are keeping him at the moment but he will be out later. We needed to see that you were all right and whether you wanted to stay somewhere else tonight," she said.

"I will phone a friend and stay there for a few days. I will be out of the house by 1:00 p.m.," I said.

"Then, we will let him out at 2:00 p.m.," she said, as she left.

I phoned Susan, packed some of my clothes and quickly left the house, just in case something went wrong and he came home early.

When I got to Susan's home, she was horrified by the way I looked. She took good care of me all weekend and we talked about what had happened. All I could think about was it was a good job Angela was not with me to see this happen.

Steve rang Susan in the evening to find out if I was with her, but she gave nothing away and was careful how

LOSS OF FAITH

she spoke to him so he would not feel we had talked.

"It looks like he is calling your friends to find you," she said.

"Well, let him. I don't want to see him yet," I replied.

It was so good to be with my friend. I felt safe and secure and she wouldn't let me do anything or go anywhere. She wanted me to be safe and looked after.

Chapter Twenty-Five

Double Betrayal

It would take some time for the bruising to go away, so I phoned in sick at work. I also needed some time to regain my strength and energy to be strong enough to see Steve again.

I was furious with him, not only for beating me, but for planning to cheat on me again.

Can I even think about taking him back?

I had to face him but was dreading it.

I had heard that he had let himself go and was spending time at his mum's and dad's house. His dad would not have given him an easy time, as he was old fashioned and strict. But I didn't care, as he deserved what he got.

Susan was a good friend and offered to set up a meeting with Steve at her house, so I would not be alone with him. On the day of our meeting, my stomach was in knots and I felt sick.

There was a knock at the door and Susan said, "He

LOSS OF FAITH

turned up on time." She opened the door not saying a word, and he walked in looking very sheepish. His mum had made him turn up clean and tidy with well ironed jeans and a T Shirt. It had to be his mum that had ironed his clothes, because Steve was hopeless at it. Susan looked at him and asked, "Well are you going to sit down?"

He never spoke as he walked to the kitchen table, pulled out a chair and sat down. There was a deadly silence.

Susan quickly said, "I am going to the living room so you two can talk. I am not far away if you need me, Patricia," and she left. That was her way of saying to Steve, "She is not alone and be careful as I am her witness."

He just sat there looking down at the table and then burst into tears, bumbling his words out. "I am so sorry Patricia. I don't know what came over me, please forgive me. I will get help. I have been to the doctor's and I am waiting to see a counsellor and I am going to Alcoholic's Anonymous. I am getting help. I know that doesn't alter what I have done, but I love you and don't want to lose you. Just give me one more chance and I will prove to you I am a good husband and can change."

I just sat back in my chair listening, my mind flitting back and forth to the memory of what happened as he talked. Not knowing whether I could trust his words or even him, I felt numb.

What should I do?

"Haven't you got anything to say to me Patricia?" Steve said with a subdued voice.

"Not really. I don't know whether, I can trust your words or even you. I have heard it all before and I know your parents would give you a hard time. So my question is, are they your words or your dad's?" I replied without feeling or emotion. I felt numb.

"Yes, my dad has gone mad with me as I had to tell them what had happened that night. I told my parents myself, because I didn't know what had come over me that night for me to do what I did. I take responsibility for it and I am ashamed of myself. Please give me another chance. I love and want you, Patricia. We can work this out," he said, panic in his voice. He talked for about two hours and I sat and listened. Maybe I was hoping he would trip himself up. I sat there waiting to pounce on one wrong word, but it never came. He was so sorry for what he had done. He cried and asked for my forgiveness. He promised it would never happen again and that he would never touch another drop of alcohol. He just wanted to be given one last chance as he did not want to lose me. He sounded so convincing. I was still numb all over, everything going through my head, feeling like I was there, but not. I didn't want another failed marriage.

"Okay I will come back home and give you one last chance. I need to pack my things so wait for me in the car," I quickly said, not really knowing whether this was the right thing to do.

Steve went to the car and Susan came back into the kitchen asking, "Are you sure this is what you want to do?"

"I have to try. I already have one failed marriage and don't want another," I replied, as I packed my clothes up to leave.

"Okay, as long as this is what you want," she said,

LOSS OF FAITH

giving me a big hug before I left.

I was not sure myself that things would be better. I was really nervous about going back, but I did. Walking into that house after what had happened was a major emotional trauma for me, but I took a deep breath and walked in with an uncomfortable feeling inside.

Steve's parents had obviously cleaned up the mess, as there were flowers on the table, a 'welcome home' card and a present wrapped in fancy paper, waiting for me.

Steve handed me the present saying, "This is for you."

I opened it and inside was a gold necklace with matching bracelet.

This is the value he puts on doing what he did?

"Thank you. It's beautiful," I said, not daring to say anything else, just in case it upset him.

I felt nervous and sick in my stomach but I knew it was something I had to do. He was my husband and, even though I wasn't sure I could ever get over this and trust him again, I had to try.

It was not easy to be around him as the memories were so vivid. I could not stand his touching me and I was nervous when he would catch me off guard. I was always wondering on the inside whether he would do it again. It was not easy to smile on the outside and hide the pain within.

I decided to go back to work after two weeks as the bruising and swelling on my face had gone down. Since I told them I had fallen down and hurt myself, no one at work expected me to look perfect. I needed to be there and be occupied. I knew the first day would be the worst with people asking questions. After that, everyone would go about their own business. So I went back.

Steve did make an effort to change. He stopped drinking. We went for walks instead of going to the pub. He was caring and attentive. He was going to counselling and AA. Slowly, as time passed, I felt easier and more relaxed. He knew it was going to take a while for me to trust him.

A couple of months had passed and everything seemed fine. Then, Steve came home one day and suggested that we go for a drink at the local pub. My face said everything. My mouth dropped, my eyes opened in fear, my body went rigid and my stomach turned upside down.

Steve quickly said, "It will be okay. We have to go sometime." I felt I was walking on egg shells wondering when the next disaster was going to happen. Having to be careful what I said and did, I wasn't happy being like this. If only I could trust him.

"I know," I replied tentatively, wondering whether he would have a pint of beer or a soft drink.

I reluctantly went with him, and the night went well, even though my fear was overwhelming, scared to say or do anything wrong, in case the incredible demon came out.

Over the next three months, we started to go out more and had a good time. Steve seemed to have gotten himself under control and my fears subsided. But still, there was this nagging doubt in the back of my mind.

Six months had passed since the incident, and everything seemed to be going well between us, except for one thing—my work.

I was very good at my job and that's where I felt most

LOSS OF FAITH

secure. Due to my efforts, I gained another promotion with more money. I could do no wrong. I was climbing the ladder where no other woman had gone before. It appeared that I was fighting for women's rights, because I had to work four times harder than a man to prove my abilities.

While I gained respect from my bosses, I also felt jealousy from both men and women. So, both my work and personal life were battles, but in very different ways. I loved working and proving that I could do things because this opened doors for other women to follow.

Unfortunately, this became a problem for Steve. He did not like my gaining promotions or more money. When we went to work functions and he had to listen to all the praise and respect I was given by my colleagues, he became angry and jealous.

What was I doing wrong to cause this? For once in my life, I just wanted to feel normal.

My intuitive senses were becoming heightened and I could feel Steve changing and pulling away from me, no matter what I did to please him. I could sense that something was about to happen, and nothing I could do would change it.

One morning, I went to work with a bad feeling, as though my world was coming to an end. I just could not push those thoughts away. It festered inside me like a virus taking over my body. Anxiety set in and I began to feel faint and sick.

My boss came into my office and asked, "Can you come with me now? I have called a meeting to talk about production costs."

LOSS OF FAITH

This was just what I needed to take my mind off this terrible feeling inside.

At this meeting, all of my senses were back in full flow. I knew what everyone was going to say before they said it, and I felt very strange.

Suddenly, I had a vision of Steve with one of my friends in our bed at our house. Panic set in and I fainted.

When I came round, everyone was standing over me.

"Are you all right, Patricia?" my boss asked.

"Yes, I think so," I replied.

"You have been working so hard. It's time for you to go home and rest," he said.

"Yes, I will just have a cup of tea and then go home. I am very tired," I replied.

I felt really ill and wondered how I would even get home in this condition. My boss stayed with me until I left. Then, the strangest thing happened. When I got into my car, I stopped feeling sick and I felt okay.

All the way home my stomach was in knots. I hoped my vision was wrong because I was not sure how I would cope or what I would do.

Why does this happen to me? I am a lovely, giving person that does no one any harm.

Tears started streaming down my face and I knew that the bad feeling I had and my vision could not be wrong, but I so desperately did not want to believe it.

I arrived home to find two cars on the driveway. My heart sank and I sat in my car for a few minutes in panic.

What am I going to do?

At that moment, a feeling of calm and strength flooded through my body. I jumped out of my car, unlocked the

LOSS OF FAITH

house door, headed straight for our bedroom and opened the bedroom door. There, in front of me, was my husband and one of my so-called friends, having sex in our bed. They both looked up at me horrified, and I said nothing.

I stood very calm just looking at them for a few seconds and nobody moved. Suddenly, I had the strength of ten men. I picked up the side of the bed with them in it and turned it upside down so they landed stark naked on the floor with the bed on top of them.

I opened the window, picked up all of their clothes and threw them outside, into the garden below. I then went to our wardrobe, grabbed all of Steve's clothes and threw them out of the window. I just saw red, and my heart was racing with anger, hurt, anxiety as tears rolled down my face like a waterfall.

By this time, they were both surfacing stark naked from under the bed.

I said very calmly, "You two, get out of my house and my life, forever! Tomorrow, I'm going to see a solicitor and start divorce proceedings. So, just get out and don't even try to say one word."

I walked out of the bedroom, into the lounge, and sat very poised and calm, although on the inside I was shaking like a leaf and panicking.

I could hear them scurrying like rabbits out of the back door, in broad daylight, to pick up their clothes and then come back inside to get dressed. I heard Steve say, "Don't worry, I will sort it out with her." Then, she left.

Steve walked into the lounge and said, with a worried tone in his voice, "We need to talk."

"I don't think so." I said. "You will have to leave and

go to your parents, as I am divorcing you and there is nothing to talk about except through a solicitor. This is the last thing you will ever do to me. All I can say to you is 'goodbye.' So, please leave as there is nothing more to say or do," I replied.

Steve just stood there.

"Please go. My mind is made up and there is nothing more to say," I said, standing up, walking to the back door and opening it for him to go.

"Are you sure this is what you want?" he asked.

"I have never been so positive in my life, so please just go. There is no turning back. I will see a solicitor tomorrow and start divorce proceedings," I replied looking at him straight in his eyes and extending my hand for him to exit the house.

He walked out, picked up his clothes from the back garden, loaded them in the car and drove away.

After he left, I just collapsed. I hated who I was. My feelings and visions were a curse. I just wanted to be normal and not always know what was going to happen ahead of time.

"Everything will be all right for you, Patricia," a voice said.

"Oh, just go away and leave me alone. I hate you. I don't want anything more to do with you. You just give me more and more pain. I can't take anymore," I screamed.

I ran into the spare bedroom, fell onto the bed, sobbed my heart out, and eventually, fell asleep.

Chapter Twenty-Six

Refuge from the Storm

When I woke up, it was daylight. I thought I had just been asleep for a few hours. The phone rang and it was my boss, asking me how I was. It was the next day and I had slept for about fifteen hours.

I told him everything. He was very understanding and told me to take as much time off as I needed.

I phoned my solicitor and made an appointment to see him at the end of the day. I was determined to set my divorce in motion. I also knew I could not stay at the house because I could not stop the visions from coming back and showing me what had happened.

What am I going to tell my parents?

I spent the day with my thoughts and fears and kept myself busy cleaning and tidying the house. I couldn't face talking to anybody or seeing anybody. I just wanted to be alone. I felt like Death warmed up.

I went to see the solicitor. He was a bald, rotund man

and he looked at me over his glasses as I walked into his office. His room was filled with books and his desk was very untidy. I remember on the floor behind his desk were piles of files. As I entered the room, I noticed a window on the left which looked over the town. I felt very comfortable with him.

After the usual pleasantries, he said, "You could sell the house, sort out your finances and do a legal separation first. That way things would be set into motion."

"I think that's the right way to go," I told him. After leaving his office, I quickly went to the estate agent's office to put the house on the market. The agent was going to send things to Steve to sign as well, because many forms required our joint signatures.

Then I returned home, packed up my things, put them in the car and then dropped the keys off at the estate agent's office. I was nervous as I drove to my parents' house because I knew what Mother would say.

When I arrived, I sat in the car for a few moments.

Here we go again.

My heart filled with anxiety and my stomach started churning.

I finally got the courage to get out of the car and go inside.

"What are you doing here?" Mother asked in a questioning voice.

Father took one look at me and said, "I told your mother last night that I saw you coming home with suitcases. Are they in the car?" he asked.

"Yes, Father, they are," I replied.

"Then, you must have good reasons to be here. Let's

go and get your things out of the car and put them in your bedroom. We can talk later," he said, as he got up, took me by the arm and walked me to the car.

I was puzzled. No questions and no arguments from Mother.

What was going on?

After I sorted out my things in the bedroom, I came downstairs.

"Make the girl a cup of tea, Mother," Father said.

Mother got up without saying a word, which was strange, and went into the kitchen to make the tea.

"Come and sit with me, Patricia, and let's talk," Father said.

I walked over and sat in the arm chair next to him.

"Patricia, I know you have been unhappy for a long time, so tell me, what has happened?" he asked.

Mother brought in a cup of tea for Father and me and said, "I am going to the shops," and then she left.

Very strange.

"It's okay, Patricia. I have sorted out your mother to give us a chance to talk," Father said.

I told him everything that had happened from start to finish, which raised tears and emotions. He just sat there, intently listening to my story.

After I had finished, he looked at me with his loving eyes asking, "Why did you put up with this for so long? Why did you not come home? Your happiness is our happiness, you know, and I have sensed for a long time that you were not happy."

"I wanted to make my marriage work. I just can't seem to make a personal relationship last. What is wrong

LOSS OF FAITH

with me?" I asked, bursting into tears

"Nothing is wrong with you. You just chose the wrong person, that's all. The main thing now is that you are home, safe, and have time to recover and start again. He will not bother you here," Father said.

His words made me feel warm and safe. I loved my father and he always seemed to say the right things when I needed to hear them most.

Mother came back from the shops and nothing was said. This was new behavior for her. I knew Father would tell her everything when I was not around, but that did not matter as long as she left me alone.

Chapter Twenty-Seven

Look Away from the Light

The next couple of days at my parents' home were quiet and I returned to work.

Everything started up again when Steve received things regarding the divorce. He phoned me and was mad. He thought everything would work out and that we would get back together.

He could not understand that he was in the wrong and that I just could not take it anymore.

Money was an issue for him and he began arguing about what was his. All I could say to him was that he would have to talk to his solicitor. I did not want to see or talk to him again and I told him to leave me alone, but he would just not stop.

What can I do?

One day the phone rang and Father answered it. I just knew it was Steve. My heart was in a panic and I just wanted to run away. I couldn't hear what father was saying as my mind was racing and my emotions overwhelmed me. When Father hung up, he turned, looked at me and said, "He won't be bothering you again, so you can stop jumping every time the phone rings."

My face always showed everything, absolute relief. I was getting fed up with the hassle and I just wanted it all to go away, so I was thankful to my father for his help.

"You forget, Patricia, you are not in this on your own," he said.

"I know, Father, but it is not always easy. You try to sort things out yourself and not bring others into it. I just thought he would give up by now and go away, but I was wrong," I replied.

After that, I never had another phone call from Steve, but the papers that came through the solicitors were petty and about money. So much so, that even my solicitor had to laugh at what was coming to him. One of the items of dispute was his car, which did not have a stereo, and mine did. Even though his car was more expensive than mine, he wanted the price of a stereo so he could put one into his car. He didn't get that money.

The house was eventually sold and we got our finances sorted out and settled. The legal separation was put into place. So now, I was finally free to get on with my life.

It helped that work was busy. I was doing a great deal of travelling with my job. I was away from home during the week and back home on the weekends. This made it easier to cope with my mother and staying in her house.

She still saw me as a child and would not give me a key to the door. I had to be home by 10:30 p.m. At twenty-five years of age, that was a bit much. It caused a lot of arguments, and I knew I could not stay long term with my parents.

My job changed and I was working close to home, so I had to change my life. I could not keep living with my parents. I had to get on my own feet and get away from the entrapment of my mother.

My brother was in the RAF at Scampton, so I started visiting him on the weekends to get a break from home.

It was there that I met Hamish. He was so much fun. He was a fireman in the RAF and played rugby. He was built like a rugby player, stocky, with a great sense of humour. We got on well and after a couple of months we started seeing each other every weekend. After about three months of these weekend visits, we planned a holiday to Scotland to see his parents.

We drove to his parents' home in my car. It was a long journey to Scotland, but we took it slowly, stopping for something to eat and drink. The journey seemed endless and I was getting tired, as we went in my car and I was driving. When we arrived, his parents had made dinner for us. They were lovely people and were very interested in knowing everything about me. It did feel a bit like an interrogation.

At the dinner table one night, Hamish's father said, "We were quite surprised when we met you, as you are not like his other girlfriends. You are beautiful, intelligent and an amazing person. We can see that you make our son very happy. We are pleased to have you as part of our family."

"Thank you so much. That is so kind of you," I replied, feeling embarrassed and blushing.

LOSS OF FAITH

Hamish just looked at me and smiled.

The holiday went far too quickly, as Scotland is a beautiful place, lots of hills and valleys, lakes and plenty of greenery and nature. It was so peaceful and tranquil. I hadn't been to Scotland in a long time and the energy was perfect for relaxing and gaining my strength. It had been a lovely time and his parents had made me feel so welcome.

The morning we were leaving, I woke up with a bad feeling. Oh no, not again.

Hamish put our bags in the car and both his parents came out to see us off. They gave me a big hug and said, "Don't be a stranger. You are welcome anytime. Hamish, you make sure that you bring her back to see us."

"I will Dad," he replied.

We got in the car and drove away, waving to his parents as we left, heading for home. It was a long and tiring journey and we needed to make frequent stops.

When we stopped the second time at a Little Chef eating place, the bad feeling grew worse, so much so, that I did not want to move. We went in and ordered our food and drinks, and while we were eating the bad feeling was growing and growing.

How could I explain this to Hamish? He did not know anything about this side of me and he would think I was crazy.

I sat, longer than normal, just mulling things over in my mind.

What could it be?

Suddenly, Hamish said, "We better get a move on if we are going to get home in the daylight."

"Okay," I said, getting up. My heart was in my mouth.

LOSS OF FAITH

I just did not want to move but I had to. I could not explain anything to him because he just would not understand.

We set off, picked up the dual carriageway, and headed for home.

I was driving within the speed limit, in the right hand lane, just going with the traffic flow. The dual carriageway was very busy and that bad feeling kept getting worse.

Suddenly, a tractor/trailer pulled out of a right hand road and drove straight across the two lanes in front of me. The traffic was swerving to miss it, but I had no place to go. It was all in slow motion. I geared down and stepped on the brakes, but there was nothing I could do except watch it happen in slow motion, until my car hit the trailer. I was knocked out.

When I came round, Hamish was out of the car and at my side, shouting my name. I looked up to see the steering wheel in my chest. I could not feel my legs.

There was no chance of my getting out of the car as I was trapped by the steering wheel. People crowded round the car talking to me, trying to keep me awake. Someone gave me a cup of sweet tea for shock.

A doctor arrived as he was in the traffic behind me. He kept talking to me, asking me questions and feeling my pulse. "The fire brigade and ambulance are on the way," he said.

It seemed like a lifetime before they arrived. I was beginning to panic and the doctor was trying to stop me from going into shock.

The ambulance arrived first and the medical personnel came straight over, held my hand and asked me questions to keep me calm, while the fire engine turned up.

LOSS OF FAITH

I kept looking in front of me.

I should be dead. There was no way anyone could have survived this crash.

"You will walk out of this with cuts and bruises," a voice said.

No way.

I could not feel my legs and my chest was beginning to hurt. I heard the doctor say he was worried about the pain in my chest and that my blood pressure was very unstable. He was worried that I would have a heart attack. I was beginning to panic and fear the worst.

Everyone was trying to get me to breathe slowly when I could hardly breathe at all. The ambulance men kept giving me oxygen. I thought I was going to die, as I kept drifting in and out of consciousness.

In my lucid moments, I could see angels around the car, holding my hand and talking to me. One was in the car with me, telling me everything would be all right. Another angel took me out of my body and stood with me as I looked at my car with my body in it. I could see everything that was happening, but I felt very calm.

I watched the fire engine arrive and the firemen looking at the car and talking to me, telling me what they were going to do. They had to cut the car roof off, and cut the side of the car, to be able to release the seat and get me out.

"This is going to take some time, but we will work as fast as we can," the firemen said.

Hamish didn't move from my side of the car, trying to hold my hand and not get in the way at the same time. I could hear panic in his voice as he kept saying "Patricia" to keep me awake.

LOSS OF FAITH

They turned on their equipment and started cutting. By this time, I did not care. I was so frightened. The one thing I did not want to do was live, if I had to lose my legs. That was all I could think about. Fear just flooded through my body.

The angels kept reassuring me that everything would be all right and that I would walk out with only cuts and bruises, but I did not believe them. I had lost all trust in them, and believed they were there, just waiting for me to die.

Everything seemed to take forever, and I was getting so weak. I could hear the doctor in the distance saying that he was getting worried about my blood pressure. Everything seemed to be against me.

Just let me die.

"You are not going to die," Merlin said.

"Is that you, Merlin?" I asked

"Yes, Patricia. Don't worry, I am here. You will be all right. I am here to give you strength and the will to live," he said.

"But, I am so weak, Merlin," I replied.

"Just open your eyes and hold my hand, Patricia. I am right by your said," he said.

I opened my eyes and there was Merlin, in the car with his flowing, colourful robes and long beard.

"I love you, Merlin, but I am so tired," I replied.

At that moment, everything was moving. I realized that I was being pulled out of the car, placed on a stretcher and put into the ambulance, which left the scene at high speed, with its light flashing and siren blaring.

The ambulance men were attending to me, giving me

oxygen and checking my pulse.

It was as though I was in some sort of void. I could vaguely hear the ambulance men say they were concerned about me, as I was drifting in and out of consciousness and my blood pressure was through the roof.

I could see Merlin and angels all around me. The ambulance was filled with angelic beings that placed their hands on my body and told me that everything was going to be fine.

I could see a strong white light which was pulling me towards it. Merlin kept saying, "Look away from the light, Patricia."

"But I am so tired, Merlin," I replied.

"No, Patricia, stay awake and away from the light. Have strength to keep awake. You are much needed in this life. Think of your daughter, who you love so much. She will need you in this life," he said.

"My daughter, Merlin, where is she?" I asked.

I could hear the ambulance men ask, "Who is she talking to? There is no one here."

"I am talking to God's helpers," I replied.

"It's all right, Patricia, we are nearly at the hospital," the ambulance man replied.

At that point, the ambulance came to a sudden stop and the back doors flung open. A team of people pulled me out and placed me onto a trolley. I could see their faces in a mist and behind them were all of my angelic beings. I could feel the doctors and nurses touching me but I had no idea what they were doing as I was totally out of it.

I remember looking at the ceiling, seeing angelic faces and lights as we moved down each corridor and suddenly

LOSS OF FAITH

entering a room where the doctors were. This room also was full of mist, angelic beings and swirling lights, all the colours of the rainbow. It was so beautiful and peaceful.

I was taken for x-rays and hooked up to some sort of machine. I was so scared because I could not feel anything from the waist down. But the angelic beings who stayed with me gave me constant reassurance that everything was going to be fine.

How can I believe them? I had pushed them away for such a long time. Why are they here now? I really do not want to survive especially if I am paralyzed from the waist down. I just want to sleep but these beings will not let me.

The following thoughts kept popping into my head:

What will my daughter do, if I die? She will never get to know me. I will never be able to help her, or see her get married and have kids.

These thoughts just kept circling my brain.

I must keep going for my daughter.

Everything, after that, was a blur.

Chapter Twenty-Eight

Miracle Do Happen

I woke up to daylight and the scurrying of people in my hospital room. "What is going on?" I asked.

"Oh, you're awake. Don't worry, we are getting ready for the doctor to arrive," the nurse said.

I was dreading the doctor's visit as I did not want bad news. My heart was racing with anticipation. I always thought the worst, so if it was good news, it would be a surprise.

The door to my room opened and in walked the doctor, along with what looked like a group of student doctors. They put my x-rays up and all started discussing me as if I were not there. I could not understand half of what they were saying. I was very tired and started to fall asleep.

I could hear the doctors' voices in the background as I was slowly drifting into sleep.

"Everything is going be fine, Patricia," Merlin said.

Merlin, is that you?

"Yes, Patricia. You have nothing to worry about. Just

wait and see," he said, with calmness in his voice,

I hope so, Merlin, because I am so scared.

"You have nothing to be scared of Patricia, I am here," he said.

I felt his hand on mine and a feeling of safety moved through my body. No more was said, as we did not need to say anything. There was a real strong connection between us and I trusted him. I felt this great sense of calmness and knew that he was sending me healing as tremendous energy and peacefulness came over me.

Suddenly, I could feel someone's hand on my arm and hear someone ask, "Are you awake, Patricia?"

It made me jump and I opened my eyes quickly and said, "What?"

"It's the doctor and he wants to talk to you, Patricia," the nurse said.

"Oh, okay," I replied, as my heart started beating fast.

When my eyes came into focus, there was the doctor, the student doctors and a police woman, all around my bed. It felt like being a monkey in a cage, with everyone standing in their white coats and uniforms looking at me.

"Well, Patricia," the doctor said.

I was waiting for the bad news and my stomach was churning. I heaved a big sigh, expecting the worst.

"We have looked at your x-rays and been shown the photographs by the police. It's a miracle that you are still alive. All the evidence of the crash, and the condition you were in when you came into the hospital, indicate that you should have not survived. But, all we can find are cuts and bruises. It really is a miracle," he said.

I could not believe what I heard. I was shocked and

LOSS OF FAITH

relieved both at the same time.

"So, I am all right? My legs and my chest are okay?" I asked.

"Everything is all right. You are just badly bruised with a few minor cuts. Someone was surely looking after you," he said.

"Yes, they were," I said, with a knowing look. I had seen the angelic beings and spoke with them and Merlin.

Why would they help me now when I had pushed everything away, including God and my faith?

"You have a lot of work to do, Patricia, in your lifetime and it just was not your time to go," Merlin said.

Miracles can happen then, Merlin?

"Oh yes, Patricia. You are all right now, so I have to go. We will meet again," he said, as he faded into the background.

"The policewoman wants to take a statement from you and then if you can arrange somewhere to go, we will discharge you from the hospital. There is a young man outside who has been here all night, worrying about you, so I will talk to him and let him in to see you," the doctor said.

"Thank you, doctor, that would be nice," I replied.

The doctor and his students left and the policewoman took my statement. She was also surprised that I had survived the accident. Everyone was talking about a miracle.

The policewoman left and Hamish came into my hospital room, looking totally wrecked from the car crash, and the whole experience with me and lack of sleep. His eyes were all puffed up and gray and drawn, the muscular body drooped with tiredness and fatigue. He looked so happy to see me, beaming from ear to ear. He leaned over my bed and kissed me.

"I am so happy you are fine, as I was worried about you," he said all nervous. Rugby players are not known for their softness.

"I am glad I am okay, too," I replied with relief.

"I have arranged for my parents to come and pick us up to take us back to their place to recover," he said with a smile on his face.

He was a lovely man, so kind and considerate. There was nothing for me to do except get dressed, and then I would be ready to go.

When his parents turned up they were good to me, making sure I was all right.

"We are so glad you are all right Patricia. We were so worried when Hamish phoned us to tell us what had happened and how you were," his dad said with sincerity.

"You are coming home with us and we are going to look after you and we want no arguments from you. We are happy to do it," his mother said, her eyes so deep and caring. They were both nurses, so I had to do as I was told and be looked after for a change.

They were also bossing Hamish around and telling him to do things for me. It was funny to watch him with his parents. He had been good to me and he knew how to look after me, but his parents took over the minute they arrived, and he was pushed to the back having to do what he was told.

Over the next few days, they would not let me do anything. I slept a lot, but I really wanted to get home to my parents.

LOSS OF FAITH

I had been phoning them every day but it was not the same as seeing them. I talked with Hamish and we made arrangements to go back home by train. His parents wanted me to stay, but I explained why and they were all right about it.

They drove us to the station and made sure we were on the train with all of our baggage. The journey seemed to be a long one for me. I was like a little old lady, very stiff and I could not quite stand up straight. So, Hamish had to do all the fetching and carrying.

My father met us at Doncaster train station and took us home. It had been a long journey by train from Scotland.

Father was pleased to see me. He put his arms around me and gave me a hug. I was so pleased to see him and felt secure in his arms.

"It's good to have you home safe and sound, Patricia. I can see you have been well looked after by Hamish and his parents," he said with a smile on his face. He looked at Hamish and smiled as he said, "Thank you for looking after my daughter,"

"She is worth it," Hamish replied. I could tell Father really liked Hamish with how he spoke to him. Father helped Hamish with the bags and put them in the car. It was good to be back with my father, my safety blanket. We all got into the car and headed for home.

"Mother is cooking a meal for us when we get back," Father said.

"That's nice of her," Hamish replied.

"It's the least we could do for your taking care of our precious daughter," he said. I sat quietly in the back of the

LOSS OF FAITH

car while Father and Hamish chatted away. I was watching the countryside pass by, my mind remembering the accident and what had happened.

We got back home and Father parked the car. He and Hamish unloaded the bags from the car as I walked into the house. Mother gave me a smile, as I slowly walked in, but did not speak as she was busy finishing the dinner. It smelt good. She had made one of her special meat and potato pies. So, I went and sat in the living room, while everything was taken upstairs for me to unpack later.

We all sat down in the living room and Father asked, "Mother, can we have a cup of tea?"

"Yes, I will bring it in a minute," she calmy replied.

This was not my mother. Maybe she was on her best behaviour for Hamish.

Mother brought in the tea, along with her best china with the tea pot, milk jug and sugar bowl. She placed it down, smiling as she said, "Help yourself, dinner is nearly ready."

This definitely wasn't Mother.

Father just looked at me with that knowing look and smiling, as Mother went back to the kitchen to finish the dinner.

"I'll be Mother," Father said, as he got up and poured the tea. "Help yourself to milk and sugar Hamish," he said passing the cup and saucer to him.

"Thanks," Hamish said.

Father gave me my tea as he knew how I took it and it wasn't easy for me to get up. I stared into the fire while Father and Hamish chatted. I really could not get over how Mother was behaving.

LOSS OF FAITH

She called, "Dinner is on the table."

Hamish helped me up and we all went and sat at the kitchen table, where the food smelt good and was piping hot.

"This looks good," Hamish said politely.

"Enjoy your meal," Mother replied.

Hamish was polite and waited for her to sit and start eating. Then, he tucked in.

Father wanted to know everything that had happened. He had seen the car crash in a dream, exactly the way Hamish had described it. For proof, he had told my mother about his dream and she was amazed at how accurate it had been.

In his dream, he saw me walking away from the accident, so that made him feel better, knowing that no harm would come to me.

After dinner we all relaxed in the living room and watched TV. When it was time for bed, Mother showed Hamish his bedroom and I went to mine.

"Both of you have a good night's sleep," Father said, as he went into their bedroom, Mother following.

"Will do, Father, goodnight," I replied. I was so tired my head hit the pillow and I was out like a light.

After a few days, I was beginning to feel better and needed to drive again so I would not lose my confidence.

Father agreed to lend me his car and I drove Hamish back to his barracks. I stayed with my brother overnight and then came back home.

I felt better for the drive, as that meant I could return to work and then everything could get back to normal.

Chapter Twenty-Nine

A Glimpse of Happiness

That weekend, I was sitting quietly in the living room when the telephone rang. I got up and answered it.

"Hello, this is Patricia," I said.

"It's Trevor's mum," was the reply. My whole body shook with dread, expecting bad news. "We wanted you to know that Trevor has remarried and his new wife does not want Angela. There have been lots of problems," she said in a sheepish voice. "So she is living with us now," she said with a smarmy tone.

What is she up to?

"That's not good for Angela," I replied tentatively. My heart was full of anxiety and my body was shaking all over. I was trying to contain myself so she would not hear it in my voice.

"Trevor has stopped seeing Angela and Ernest and I have talked about it and believe that one of you should see her."

I really could not believe what I was hearing.

LOSS OF FAITH

Am I misunderstanding what she is saying? They have never been nice to me, so why now? What motive do they have?

My body was trembling all over with fear and anxiety. For a few seconds, I could say nothing, absolutely dumb founded.

"Are you still there, Patricia?" she asked.

"Yes, I am, and I would be so happy to see Angela," I replied.

"Would you like to see her next weekend?" she said.

"Yes, that would be good. Shall I pick her up at 9 a.m.?" I quickly replied, before she changed her mind.

"Yes, that would be all right. Do you still have our address?" she said.

"Yes, I do. I will call for her next Saturday at 9 a.m. Thank you," I said, as I put the phone down.

I was so excited about seeing her. My mood just changed and I felt happy, excited and I began to smile.

I wonder what she looks like now? Will she like me, talk to me, will she be happy to see me?

My mind was just racing with excitement, questions, fears, anxieties, all at the same time. I flopped down in the arm chair as Father walked into the living room.

"What was that all about?" he said, looking at me.

"That was Trevor's mum. Trevor doesn't see Angela anymore as he has remarried and his wife doesn't want her. So, Angela is living with his mum and dad and they want me to start seeing her. I am picking her up next Saturday," I replied, bumbling my words out with excitement, as Mother walked in on the conversation.

"That's good news! Are you bringing her here to see us?" Father asked.

LOSS OF FAITH

"Yes, I will. I haven't decided what else I want to do, though. I don't even know how she will be with me after all this time," I replied, with hesitation in my voice.

"It will be fine, Patricia. You will see." Father replied in an understanding and calm way.

"I know, but it's been such a long time, and I keep thinking about how she was just before I gave her up," I replied in a worried tone.

"That's the past, Patricia, now it's different, you will see," he replied smiling.

I am sure he is telling me what I want to hear because he is worried as well.

I sat quietly with my thoughts and worries. Mother didn't say a thing, which was unusual. I couldn't eat or sleep with the anxiety of seeing Angela again. There was excitement, but that came with worries, too. Nobody mentioned it again all weekend. Father gave me space to sort my head out and Mother kept out of my way.

I went to work on Monday and time was going very slowly, as all I could think about was seeing Angela on Saturday. One day rolled into another, but the week could not go fast enough. I was wishing my life away.

Friday night came, and I was so excited about seeing Angela that I could not sleep. I tossed and turned all night, and I watched the clock turn to six in the morning.

So, I got up at that early hour as I did not want to be late. I had to travel to Barnsley and that was a forty-five minute drive away.

My stomach was so full of butterflies that I could not eat, so I had several cups of tea, instead. My mother and father were up but I did not say anything. I knew that Fa-

LOSS OF FAITH

ther understood and could feel what I was feeling.

Eight o'clock came and I had to leave to pick her up.

I jumped in my car and tried to keep my concentration on my driving. It was difficult as I just could not stop thinking about my daughter. The bad feelings were creeping in my stomach again, and I just could not shake them off.

Oh, just go away, please! Will she remember me? Will she want to see me? Will she hate me? Will there be deadly silence?

My mind was racing with all sorts of questions. I was so scared that she would reject me. I only wanted her happiness, but I was so nervous and frightened that she would hate me.

I did not know what she had been told about me or why I had given her up. All I knew, was it would not have been good or the truth.

I arrived at her grandparents' house and parked the car. I had a very bad feeling in the pit of my stomach. I sat for a few minutes and composed myself. Then, I got out of the car and walked up the path to the door, with the bad feeling and anxiety getting worse. As I neared the door, it opened and her grandfather stood there and said, with a smirky smiling face, "Angela does not want to go with you. She has gone out with her friends."

I could have punched him right in the face, but I restrained myself and kept my dignity.

You are not going to get to me.

"Okay, that's fine. Just tell her I will telephone her, if that is all right with you," I replied, holding back my feelings, emotions and tears.

"Oh, yes, that's all right," he said, quickly slamming the door shut in my face.

LOSS OF FAITH

He is scared of what I might do or say. I will not let you see my unhappiness. You will not get to me.

I felt angry as I walked down the path, but I could do nothing. They were totally in control of the situation. I was not in control because I had given up custody and access to my daughter. I felt so helpless but I knew I had to remain calm, otherwise, I would never get to see her.

My heart sank with pain and frustration but I managed to get into my car and hold everything together until I started the car and drove away. I was so upset that I cried all the way home. This was not a good time.

I hate them!

When I arrived home, I parked my car on the driveway and sat there for a while, trying to pull myself together. Father came out of the house to see where I was and saw me crying in the car. He got into the car with me and asked me what had happened. So, I told him everything.

"I know you want to see Angela desperately, but you know what his parents are like and they will keep doing this to you, Patricia," he said.

"I know Father, but I have to try and see her because if I don't, I will feel that I've let her down and given up an opportunity to see her. Do you understand that she is so precious to me, that I will put myself through anything if I can get the chance to spend time with her?" I cried, my tears flooding like a river and sobbing between the words trying to catch my breath. My heart was in so much pain.

How could they do this to Angela and me. Maybe she still hates me.

"I understand, Patricia. Let's go in the house and have a cup of tea," he said, as he got out of the car.

LOSS OF FAITH

We went inside and Mother asked, "Where is Angela?"

"They have told Patricia that Angela does not want to see her," Father quickly replied. This gave me a chance to pull myself together.

I was so angry with Trevor's parents for doing this to me but I knew if I lost it, they would not let me see Angela again.

The weekend passed so slowly. I could not go and see Hamish as I just wanted to cry. I spoke with him on the telephone and he understood.

I tried a few times over the weekend to contact my daughter but was constantly told that she was out. I left messages for her, but no call was returned. I did not know whether or not they were telling her about my calls, or if she just did not want to talk to me.

All this opened up old wounds and took me back to the feelings of loss that I had when I gave her up. My heart had been shattered yet again into a million pieces. I so much wanted to see her again. I loved her so much.

I could not wait to get back to work and bury my head in something constructive.

My life revolved around work, and I felt very much that I was only existing and not really living. Life without my daughter was empty.

I was so wrapped up with all this, that I did not see changes in Hamish. He got a posting abroad and we just drifted apart. It was a shame as he was a nice person, but I really was not in the right space to give to someone else.

Chapter Thirty

Letting Go, Again

I eventually got to talk to Angela by telephone through determination and the commitment to never give up. I think Trevor's parents finally gave in, as I was not going away. She was a little distant at first, but became more relaxed as we chatted over a few weeks. I didn't want to push her, I just wanted her to get to know me. Then one day, I just got the courage and blurted out, "Do you want to go swimming with me next week?" My heart was in my mouth in case she said no.

"Oh yes, I love swimming," she quickly replied.

"Then we will go next Saturday. Shall I pick you up at 9 a.m.," I said quickly, my heart racing with excitement.

"Yes, I will be ready," she replied.

We said our good-byes and put the phone down. I could not believe it! I was really going to see Angela after all this time.

We both liked swimming so that would be a fun day out. This could be the start of getting to know each other

LOSS OF FAITH

again and seeing where things would go. I could not build my hopes up too much because—knowing Trevor's parents—the ground rules could change, and Angela and I could get hurt in their game playing.

I arrived promptly at 9 a.m. on Saturday to pick up Angela. I was a little apprehensive as I walked up to the door. As it opened, Angela came running out with her things in a bag. Grandma stood at the doorway with her arms folded.

"Have her back by 6 p.m.," she snapped in a grumpy voice.

"I will," I replied as I turned and followed Angela to the car, smiling from ear to ear, my heart happy and full of excitement. We both got in the car and I drove away heading for Rotherham swimming baths. Angela was excited and chatted away in the car like we had never been apart. I just listened to her, as it was lovely to hear her voice. She was quite tall, with long blonde hair, and skinny as a rake. She really had grown up in five years. She had her own point of view and opinions. I could see a lot of me in her. Suddenly, she blurted out, "Grandma and Grandad did not want me to come today, and they were not happy when I said I was going, no matter what. They said I was just like you and I told them I was glad."

She was like me. "Well you are here now, that's all that matters," I quickly replied looking and smiling at her. On the inside I was so angry with them. I knew they would try something, but I did not want to stoop to their level and put them down. It wasn't fair to Angela to do that.

I have to make sure I do not say bad things about them.

I just wanted her to enjoy her day out with me. We

LOSS OF FAITH

went swimming and enjoyed our time together. We had water fights and played tricks on each other. She was a good swimmer and enjoyed the water slides and ball games in the pool. We could do nothing but laugh. She definitely was like me and we got on so well. After swimming, I had some additional time.

"Do you want to go and see your other Grandma and Grandad?" I asked.

"Oh yes! Please!" she replied, excited.

So we got in the car and headed for my parents' house.

My parents hadn't seen her for such a long time. They knew I was picking up Angela and that I would bring her to see them. When we arrived and pulled on the driveway, Father and Mother came and stood on the doorstep. We got out of the car and Father walked forward.

"Hello, Angela," he said holding his arms out.

Angela ran up to him, jumped in his arms, gave him a kiss, saying,"Hello!" It was as though she had never been away.

"You're all grown up now Angela," he said.

"Yes, I am," she replied.

My father put her back down and Angela ran to my mother and threw her arms around her, saying, "Hello Grandma."

Mother's face was a picture as she was taken aback. She didn't do the touchy-feely things.

"Come on in the house, Angela, and we will have something to eat and drink," she quickly said with embarrassment.

We all went into the house and sat at the kitchen table and had the food Mother had prepared. Angela never

LOSS OF FAITH

stopped talking. Father and Angela were just yapping away over dinner as though they had always been together. I was just watching in silence.

My lovely little girl. I am amazed how she has grown up. She is beautiful and intelligent.

Nothing was said or asked between us and we just enjoyed our day laughing and playing. After all, I had never really grown up and still loved to laugh. When it was time to take her home, my heart was heavy with sadness.

Why does time pass so quickly?

We said our good-byes to my parents and we got back in the car to take Angela home. We chatted all the way. Just as we pulled up outside her Grandma's house, I quickly asked,"Have you enjoyed you day out, Angela?"

"Yes, Mummy, it's been great," she replied.

Hearing her call me "Mummy" set a warm glow in my heart like the warmth of an open fire in winter.

That is the first time she called me Mummy in five years!

"Would you like to see me next Saturday?" I said, my heart in my mouth.

"Oh, yes, please! Same time" she replied.

"Okay, I'll pick you up next Saturday at 9 a.m.,"I quickly replied, my heart overwhelmed with happiness.

As I dropped Angela off at her grandparents' house, I had to remain strong and show no emotion. That was not easy for me.

I held myself together long enough to give Angela a cuddle, watch her walk into the house, and then I drove away.

Then, this overwhelming feeling of grief came over me. I had to stop the car and let the tears flow. I eventually

LOSS OF FAITH

got back home to my parents, my eyes red from crying. I managed to pull myself together to walk into the house.

"Well, Angela enjoyed herself," Father said, as I walked into the living room.

"Yes, she did, Father. I am seeing her again next Saturday," I quickly replied.

"Don't get your hopes up, Patricia, you know what her grandparents are like," he quickly replied.

"I know Father. I just want to enjoy what I have while I have it," I said.

"Well, she is all grown up now," Mother said.

"Yes, she is," I replied. This was not like Mother but she seemed to be making an effort.

"I am off to bed now. I am exhausted," I said.

"All right. Goodnight," Father said as I headed for the stairs door.

"Goodnight," I replied. I got into bed and my thoughts were just whirring round my head of the day's events. I dropped to sleep thinking of Angela. Sunday came and went. I didn't say a lot as I was thinking about Angela.

I just can't wait until next Saturday to see Angela. I am wishing my life away.

I went to work on Monday and the day and week just dragged, as I kept looking at my watch wishing Saturday would come.

Saturday did finally come and I went to pick Angela up from her grandparents' house. As I arrived, her grandfather was standing at the gate.

"There is no point getting out of your car because Angela is not here. She has gone out for the day. You will have to come back next week," he said.

LOSS OF FAITH

I was so angry inside, but I smiled sweetly and said, "Okay, that's fine. See you."

I was so mad! As I drove away, tears streamed down my face.

How dare they treat me in this way?

There was so much pain in my chest, I could hardly breathe. I managed to get home, run upstairs to my bedroom and sob my heart out.

There was a knock at my door, and Father walked in.

"What has happened, Patricia?" he asked.

I cried while I tried to explain.

"You know they will keep doing this, Patricia. They are not very nice people," he said, pulling me towards him and giving me a cuddle.

"I know Father, but I need to keep trying for Angela," I cried.

"I know, Patricia, but how much more can you keep taking yourself?" he asked.

"I don't know, but I have to try. That's all I know right now," I said, wiping the tears from my eyes.

There was so much sadness in my heart. All I wanted was to see my daughter.

"Come on, Patricia, let's go downstairs and have a cup of tea," he said.

We went downstairs in silence and sat down in the living room. I saw Mother look at me.

Father said very quickly, "Make us a cup of tea, Ada."

So, Mother went into the kitchen. I just could not face her asking a lot of questions. When I was in trouble or upset the only person I wanted was my father. I know Mother felt left out, but I just could not talk to her.

LOSS OF FAITH

Over the next six months, it was hit and miss with seeing Angela. Sometimes, they would not let me see her. Other times, I would get her for a couple of hours. Now and again, I would get her for the whole day and once, I got her for the weekend.

It's as though they were just playing with me. But this was not just about me, it was about Angela. I was getting angry and bitter towards her grandparents because of what they were doing. I had tried so hard not to let my emotions take over because one wrong move and they would stop letting me see her. They were in full control and they knew it.

As usual, I buried myself in work, and hid from the world. I just wished that it would all go away.

The pain of what was happening with Angela was festering, like an open wound, and would not let up. I was feeling down and depressed. Nothing really mattered anymore. I just could not go on feeling upset and hurt and allow someone else to control my life. This inner battle was constantly there, because I wanted things to change and to see my daughter.

My patience and faith were being tested. I was not sure how much longer I could keep doing this.

Why can't things just be simple and straight forward? Why all this hurt and pain? It is more than any one person can take. Why is it always me?

I had made arrangements to pick up Angela and take her to Sherwood Forest with some friends and their children. The kids were Angela's age. So, I went to pick her up and when I arrived, her grandparents came to the door and said I could not have her because they were taking her out.

LOSS OF FAITH

I said nothing and just left. I drove away and found somewhere quiet to park. My body was in shock. I could not cry. I was just shaking all over and my heart was pumping so fast. I was getting pains in my chest and down my arms. I became so hot that I opened the car door to get some air. I just could not move for about thirty minutes and then my body calmed down. I just sat there, not being able to move, and just stared into space. I felt numb all over.

How can I keep letting them do this to me? I love Angela, but I just cannot take this anymore. I have to let go and hope my daughter will come and see me when she is old enough to make her own choices and decisions.

About two hours had passed and I decided to drive home and talk to my father.

When I got home, I rang my friends to let them know I was not coming. My father was already in the living room and had listened to my conversation on the phone with my friends.

"Well Patricia, how much longer are you going to put yourself through this?" he asked.

"I can't go on anymore, Father. I love my daughter but I cannot deal with it any more. I am going to phone her grandparents and let them know," I replied.

"I think that is a wise decision, Patricia. I look at the unhappiness on your face and the pain and frustration in your eyes. You have to start living for you now. Life is too short. You have tried and you cannot do any more. Angela will find her own way in life and I am sure you will get to see her when she is old enough to make her own choices and decisions," he said.

LOSS OF FAITH

I knew what he was saying was right, but it was painful to accept.

"I know Father, but I am so scared she will hate me and not understand the reasons behind my actions. I don't want her to think that I don't love her, because I do," I said.

We both lapsed into silence.

Here I am again, having to make the decision to give her up and feel all the emotion that comes with it.

"I just can't shed anymore tears, Father. I am numb all over," I said.

"I know it's not easy, Patricia, but you have to get on with your life and make the best of it. I watch you every day put yourself through this with no happiness for yourself. I just want you to find someone who will love you and make you happy," he said.

"I know Father, I would like that, too," I replied.

"Would you like for me to phone Angela's grandparents?" he asked.

"No, I will do it myself, and I won't lose my temper. I will do it calmly," I replied.

I got up and moved the telephone to the bottom of the stairs so I could have a private conversation with Angela's grandparents.

Trevor's mum answered the phone.

"Hello, it's Patricia. I have decided that due to what you are doing with me over Angela, it is not good for her. Angela needs a settled life, so I am not going to see her anymore. I do not want Angela to get confused and it is in her best interest that I do not see her." I said calmly.

There was a deadly silence on the end of the telephone line. I remained polite and said, "I have to go," and put the

LOSS OF FAITH

phone down, went back into the living room and placed the telephone back on the bureau. I was shaking all over.

Father got up and cuddled me so tight. This overwhelming feeling came over me and I sobbed my heart out for about half an hour. I was so distraught with the loss of my daughter, yet again. But it was for her happiness, not mine, that I made this choice.

Chapter Thirty-One

My New Home, a Sports Car & Butterflies

All weekend, I kept to myself as I did not want to see or talk to anyone. I stayed in my bedroom and kept crying until I was exhausted and dropped to sleep. Father kept bringing me a cup of tea, without saying a word. He knew I was in distress and needed to be by myself to grieve. It was his way of checking up on me. I couldn't eat as my heart was in so much pain.

Monday came and I went to work and buried myself there.

At home, Mother kept bugging me saying in a snappy way, "Pull yourself out of it. Patricia."

That irritated me so much. She really had no idea how I felt and how difficult it was for me. She was so unfeeling, I was sure her heart was made of stone.

"Just leave me alone, you are horrible and heartless," I shouted back walking away from her. I hated her for her attitude and lack of love and understanding.

LOSS OF FAITH

My life was a mess and all she could say was, "Pull yourself together."

She could not imagine how I was feeling or what was going on inside my head. It came to a point that I could not stand it any longer. Here she was, again, driving me out of the house. I started looking for somewhere else to live.

While looking through the newspapers, I came across an advert that said, "Room to rent." I thought that maybe this was the answer, even if it was in someone's house. That meant I would not be completely on my own.

I phoned the advert and arranged to go and see the room that evening. The house was a large Victorian terraced house in a nice area of Rawmarsh, overlooking the park. Tony owned the house and lived in one room, and Patrick had the attic room. The other room was smaller, but seeing as how I was only going to be sleeping in it and sharing the rest of the house, it was big enough. Tony looked like Rod Stewart and Patrick was small with dark hair and a mustache. He was a scientist and looked like one, a little way out. Everyone was into music so that was a bonus. They made me feel welcome even at the viewing.

Everyone shared the main area of the house. They were two nice, young men with girlfriends who came to stay at the weekends. I felt very comfortable with them and they made me feel safe and welcome. So, I agreed to take the room.

Maybe this was guided into my life. I feel that this is going to change my life in some way, but how, I am not sure. What would Mother say?

I could move into the room straight away, so I could

LOSS OF FAITH

go home and move my things. The only thing I dreaded was telling my mother, who was straight-laced and behind the times.

When I got home, I took a deep breath and walked into the house.

"Where have you been?" Mother asked.

"I have been to look at a room to rent in a house, and I have taken it. So, I am here to pack and move out," I replied.

"What kind of room, and who with?" she questioned.

"It's a three bedroom house and the owner lives there and rents two rooms out," I said.

"What is her name?" Mother asked.

"It's not a 'her'—it's a 'him'. The house has two men," I quickly said.

"What?" she asked, angrily.

"You heard me, Mother," I replied.

"Bob, come in here and talk some sense into her," she shouted.

"What's going on?" Father asked.

"She is moving into a house with two men. What will the neighbours say?" Mother asked, aggravated.

Father looked at me, and asked, "Do you know what you are doing, Patricia?"

"Yes, Father, if you help me take my things down, you will see that it's a nice house and nice people. They have girlfriends who come and stay at the weekend, and I feel they will look after me. They are really nice. You and Mother can come and see," I replied.

"I am not going anywhere near that house. You should not be staying with men. It's not right," Mother snapped.

LOSS OF FAITH

"Oh, there you go again, Mother," I replied.

"I will come with you and make sure you are all right and settled in," Father said.

"Oh, taking her side again!" Mother snapped like a broken old bullfrog.

"I am not taking anyone's side. I just want to see the house and meet the people to settle my mind that she will be all right," Father said, raising his voice and turning his head to look at her with an expression that meant he was truly annoyed.

Mother went completely silent. I went upstairs and packed my things and Father helped me load them into both of our cars. Then, we set off for my new home.

When we got there, Tony and Patrick helped us unload the cars and get my things into my bedroom. Father had a look around the house and then sat down to have a cup of tea with us.

"Your daughter will be all right with us. We will look after her. We won't let any harm come to her," Tony said, and Patrick agreed.

"That's good to hear as I think a great deal about my daughter. But, I feel that you are both nice people and that she will be all right with you. If I didn't, I would take her home," Father replied, smiling and sitting back in the chair in a relaxed posture.

We all had a good chat and I could see that Father was comfortable. After about two hours, he said, "I'd better go, Patricia."

I walked him to his car and he gave me a big cuddle saying, "You will be fine here. You are right. They are nice people. I will come and see you here from time to time

LOSS OF FAITH

but I know your mother won't come. I will talk to her and she will get used to the idea, but we both know she won't come. Maybe you can bring the men up to our house so your mother can get used to them. Then, we can see."

"Okay, when I am settled in, I will do that," I replied.

Father got into his car and headed home and I went back inside my new home, which felt good to me.

Tony had cooked a meal and we all sat round the dining room table eating and having a glass of wine, just getting to know more about each other. It felt really comfortable, as if I had known them for a long time and they felt the same about me.

On Monday morning, we all got up and went to work. We had set a list—for who did what—and it was very much a family atmosphere. So, I was happy with the choice I had made.

We all had the same sense of humour. We liked the same things and we were all into music. I had an electric keyboard. Patrick had a guitar and Tony liked drums, but didn't have any. So we spent our evenings during the week, playing and singing music together.

We all put money into the kitty and enjoyed brewing homemade wine. We agreed (when it was ready) that we would throw a party. At the weekends, their girlfriends came and stayed, and we all went out together to the pubs and clubs, dancing and having fun. We all got on so well.

If anyone showed interest in me, they got grilled by Tony and Patrick, and if they did not like them, they would send them away. It was like having two more brothers. They really did look after me. Their girlfriends found it really funny.

LOSS OF FAITH

For the first time, I felt really happy, relaxed and at peace with myself and my life.

Even at work, people were commenting on how different I was. Suddenly, life was good and full of fun and laughter. I really had not been like this in a long time. I felt sixteen again.

The lads knew a lot of people and would suddenly ask people to come round and throw a party after we had been out. The house would be full of people and the party would always finish about 3:00 a.m.

One Saturday after everyone had gone, Patrick said, "Anyone fancy having breakfast in Scarborough?"

Because Scarborough was only a two hour drive away, I had been there many times before and I liked the beaches of this picturesque seaside resort.

"Yes!" both Tony and I replied. So we all piled into Patrick's car and set off. When we got there, the sun was just rising and we walked along the beach, took off our shoes and paddled in the sea, while we waited for the café to open. As soon as they put out its open sign, we walked in and ordered a full English breakfast—eggs and bacon, sausage, black pudding, tomatoes, beans, mushrooms, fried bread, hash browns, toast and tea. We could do nothing but laugh and tell jokes.

People must think we are mad.

After breakfast, we got in the car and drove all the way home. When we arrived we were all shattered and just went to our own bedrooms and slept the rest of the day.

All these crazy things I did not do as a teenager, I am doing now.

LOSS OF FAITH

We all went back to work a bit bleary eyed on Monday. The week flew by as did all the weeks at the house with the lads.

On Saturday I was going to visit my parents, when Patrick said, "Can I come with you? My girlfriend, Pam, is not coming until tonight."

"Sure you can," I replied.

So we got in my car and set off to my parents.

I wonder what mother will say and do.

When we got there and walked into the living room, Father looked up and said, "Hello, Patrick, come and sit down, and Mother will make you a cup of tea."

"Hello," Patrick said, sitting down.

"How would you like your tea?" Mother asked on her best behaviour.

"White with one sugar, please," he replied.

It is not as bad as I thought it was going to be.

We all sat talking and the conversation flowed. I suddenly looked at my watch and it was 6 p.m. "We had better go, Patrick, you have to pick up your girlfriend at 7:30 p.m. from the train station," I said, getting up.

"Oh, is it that time? It's gone so fast. It's been lovely to see you both. I have enjoyed my time here," Patrick quickly said as he got up.

"Well, don't be a stranger," Father replied as we walked out of the living room to the car. Mother and Father stood at the door, waving goodbye as I reversed the car off the driveway to go home.

"I hope you will let me come again with you, Patricia. It's been a good afternoon," Patrick said.

"You can come anytime you want. You heard what

LOSS OF FAITH

my father said," I quickly replied. I drove straight to Rotherham train station so Patrick could pick up Pam and we all went home.

Patrick started coming to my parent's house on a Saturday so he could look at my car. Mother used to talk to him and make him cups of tea. Mother was stubborn. She would not admit she liked him but all her actions said otherwise. Father said Patrick had a soft spot for me but I would just laugh, as he never made a move on me. He was just like a brother.

For the first time in my life, two nice people were looking after me, and it felt good.

Father used to drop in at the house to see us. He liked seeing me, but also, Tony and Patrick. Father commented that he had never seen me look so good and happy. I was positively beaming and there was definitely something different about me. I could sense it, and people were so different towards me.

I started to dress and do my hair differently. This was the "new me," ready to take on the world and carefree. I had the odd boyfriend, but if he was not liked by Tony and Patrick, he was scared off, so to speak. This really was the best time of my life.

In being happy, my faith seemed to re-appear and so did my psychic abilities. I had dreams that would come true. I had feelings that something would happen, and it did. I would just know things without being able to explain why, and I would be right. I would have 'out of body' experiences. I started doing some readings and healing work in the evenings and weekends, and my abilities were growing stronger and stronger. Everything just

LOSS OF FAITH

came together and felt so right.

I was not afraid anymore. I was comfortable with the person I had become. I liked and loved myself. I had really found the real me and it felt good. I was not looking over my shoulder at what had happened to me in the past and the hurt and pain that I carried. I found myself living for now and enjoying each day as it comes. I stopped worrying about what was going to happen.

Seeing the advertisement for the room to rent certainly had been guided. No matter how long I stayed here in the house with Tony and Patrick, it was truly the right place at the right time and was just what I needed then. I had to be thankful for what they had done for me. Getting your life back and finding yourself again is such a precious gift. It gave me a second chance at life.

My car started acting up and I wanted to change it. I asked my brother to come and look at a car with me that I had seen in a garage. It was a sports car.

Just what the doctor ordered.

I had always wanted a sports car, and now I could afford one. My brother and I went to have a look at the car and we took it for a test drive.

The salesman could not keep his eyes off me and it was embarrassing. He did give me a good deal though and I bought the car. It was so good to drive my sports car. You could not keep me out of it. I took the lads out one by one—as it was a two seater—and they enjoyed being seen in it.

About two weeks after buying the car, I got a call from the salesman, Bill, enquiring how the car was going, generally chatting, and booking it in for its first service.

LOSS OF FAITH

I took the car in for service and Bill was waiting for me. He paid me lots of attention and made sure I had a cup of tea and lots of conversation while the car was being worked on.

When the car was ready, I paid and was just about to leave and say thank you, when Bill said, "Would you like to come out with me tonight for something to eat?"

"Yes, okay," I replied.

"I'll pick you up at 8 p.m. I have your address from the purchase of your car," he replied.

"All right I will be ready," I quickly said my stomach full of butterflies with excitement.

He was cute and he did seem nice.

I left the garage with my stomach churning, all excited like a sixteen year old, but it felt good. I could not stop smiling.

I went home and the lads kept looking at me and quizzing me about what I was smiling about.

"I am going on a date tonight," I said.

"Who is it? Where did you meet him?" they both said, at the same time.

"I went to buy a car, and came out with a car and a date," I replied.

"So, you don't know much about him. Do you want us to come with you and find out about him? I don't like the sound of this," Patrick said.

"I will be fine on my own. It's nice that you worry but really, I will be fine and I won't be late, so you can stay up and meet him," I replied.

"Okay, Tony and I will wait up for you to make sure you get back home safe," Patrick said.

LOSS OF FAITH

I knew they would worry, so waiting up for me was a compromise.

Time went so slowly, as it always does when you want something, but I got myself ready and waited for Bill to turn up.

"You look really nice tonight, but you will be careful and don't let him touch you," Patrick said.

"It is the first date, so I am unlikely to let anything happen. Don't worry, I will be fine," I replied.

Just then a car pulled up outside, and it was Bill.

"He is here, so I am off. See you," I said, as I hurried out the door. Out of the corner of my eye, I saw both Tony and Patrick jump up and head for the window to have a look. That put a smile on my face as they did really care about me.

Bill looked pleased to see me as I got into the car. My heart was racing like a school girl, going on her first date. He was tall, handsome, slim and smartly dressed in a navy blue suit, white shirt and matching tie, with deep blue eyes.

He was very easy to talk to and made me feel at ease. We went for a drive and found a country pub to have a meal.

I remember that night as though it were yesterday. It was an old pub with beams, low romantic lights and an open log fire burning in the corner of the room.

We sat at a table near the open fire. While Bill was talking to me across the table, a white mist appeared around us and an angel appeared and stood smiling. I felt such a sense of peace and happiness. Everything, for just a few moments, did not move, not even the flames of the fire. It

LOSS OF FAITH

just looked like I was standing in a photograph. Time literally had stood still for everything and everybody around me but I could move and so could the angel.

She looked at me, smiled and said, "Enjoy your time for however long it lasts."

What do you mean?

She disappeared without answering and everything returned to normal.

Chapter Thirty-Two

Brotherly Love & Whirlwind Romance

"Are you all right, Patricia," Bill asked.

"Oh yes, I was just wondering where the toilets were, so I will go and find them," I said, getting up from the table.

I had to say something and this seemed to be the best option. I could go to the toilet and pull myself together. I could not explain to Bill what had just happened because I did not know him that well, and he would probably not understand, and would think I had lost my marbles.

I kept thinking about what the angel had said and wondered what it meant.

I just wish she had stayed a little longer to tell me more. I hate not knowing.

I went back to the table as Bill was waiting. He could do nothing but look at me as I walked back towards him.

As I sat down, he said, "You looked like an angel from heaven as you were walking."

LOSS OF FAITH

"Thank you," I said.

Where did that come from?

I just could not stop thinking about all of this.

Come on Patricia, pull yourself together, you are in good company.

We seemed to have been talking for hours when Bill asked, "Do you want to go for a drive or go home?"

"What time is it?" I asked.

"It's 9:30," he replied.

"Let's go for a drive. It's still early," I said.

Bill paid for the meal and we set off driving.

"I know a nice place where we can park the car and walk by the lake, if you would like that?" he asked.

"Yes, that would be good," I replied.

"Okay, we will go then. It is more or less on our way home," he said.

"It sounds lovely," I replied.

We pulled up at the lake. It was a clear evening with the full moon shining high in the sky and sending shimmers of light across the lake. It was both beautiful and romantic.

We set off walking slowly, enjoying the scenery. Bill was a perfect gentleman and did not try anything. He just held my hand.

"I have really enjoyed the evening and your company Patricia," he said.

"Thank you. I have enjoyed tonight and your company too," I quickly replied.

It was so quiet and peaceful by the lake. The view was amazing, just like a picture postcard. We didn't need to talk as we slowly walked round the lake, as the moment was so beautiful, so romantic.

"What time is it Bill," I asked quietly. "It's 10:15 p.m." he replied, looking at his watch.

"I had better go home as it will be late when I get back," I said, feeling disappointed the time had gone so quickly, but I had made a promise to the lads not to be too late.

"Okay, if that's what you want" he said, sounding disappointed, as we headed for the car.

"It's just that I have to get up for work early in the morning," I quickly replied.

"I know, it's all right," he said.

We got in the car and Bill put on the radio and the DJ was playing love songs. We didn't speak on the way home, we both liked the same music and it was just right for the occasion. It was the Carpenters. I so loved their music.

I got home about 11:00 p.m. As the car pulled up at the front door, I said, "Thank you Bill for a lovely evening."

"I have had a lovely evening too. I will ring you tomorrow," he replied as I got out of the car. He watched me walk into the house and then drove away.

True to form, Tony and Patrick were waiting up for me, watching the television.

"Well? Did you have a good evening and did he try anything with you?" Patrick asked.

"I had a good evening and no, he did not try anything. He is nice," I replied.

"Anyway, I am off to bed now—goodnight," I said walking upstairs. My heart was racing with excitement

LOSS OF FAITH

and there was a spring in my step. I was so happy. I felt really good.

I could hear the lads saying goodnight in the distance.

My head was floating on clouds. I could not stop thinking about the evening and whether Bill would ring me the next day. I tossed and turned all night thinking about the night's events.

The alarm went off and it was time to get up and go to work.

It seemed like a long day as I did not get a phone call. I had given him my work number, but nothing. A sense of sadness crept in and I began to think he was not interested.

I got home about 6:30 p.m. and was feeling really flat and disappointed. As I closed the front door, the telephone rang. I picked it up and it was Bill. It was surprising how my heart started to flutter.

"I am working until 7:30, but would you like to go out about 8:30?" he asked.

"Yes, that would be nice," I replied.

"I'll pick you up then at 8:30. Have to go. I have customers. See you later," Bill said, as he hung up the phone.

My heart pounded with anticipation.

Not much time to sort myself out and get myself looking good after work. Has my life begun to change for the better?

I quickly got ready and Bill landed exactly on time. I got in the car and we went out to a local pub for drinks and something to eat.

"You look lovely tonight, Patricia, but you look lovely every time I see you," he said looking at me with his deep blue eyes.

LOSS OF FAITH

"Thank you," I replied, blushing. It was like I was up in the clouds floating. I had never felt like this before. We just talked and talked. We had so much in common. The time just flew by, and it was time to go home again.

My dreams and my intuition were showing me—moving home, changing my job and getting married—but I just could not see it yet. It was early, and I dare not believe what I was being shown.

Bill was very enthusiastic about our relationship. He was very attentive and wanted to see me every day. He complimented me on the way I looked and bought me presents. In fact, he was sweeping me off my feet.

He made me feel really good. It was like a whirlwind had hit me and I was being pulled with the force of the wind. Not that I minded, as he was attractive and easy to talk to. He made me feel so special and I really did look forward to seeing him and spending time with him.

There was a real glow about me that everyone noticed. The lads sat me down one night before I went to bed.

Patrick said, "We are both happy for you, but we are cautious about him as he is rushing things and we don't want you to get hurt."

"I know, and I am being careful, and I appreciate your concerns. Let's see what happens," I replied getting up and going upstairs to bed. They were such a support to me and I was glad they were in my life.

I was doing well at work and getting promotions and now my personal life was beginning to change. Love and happiness were knocking at my door for the first time in a long time.

LOSS OF FAITH

My heart was beating like a thousand drums. I felt alive and happy. Bill was certainly what the doctor had ordered and I felt that I was being looked after from above. My faith and trust in God were strong and I was so thankful for the happiness and success I was experiencing. I was also using my abilities to help others. Everything seemed so perfect.

Is this what I have been looking for all my life?

Chapter Thirty-Three

Simply Perfect

My life felt so good, but I was so scared that it was all a dream. I was afraid that I would wake up to find everything had changed, that my fleeting glimpse of happiness had gone.

Could it be different this time and true love and happiness would stay with me?

I could not help but ask if this would remain in my life forever. Things were moving fast with Bill. One day when we were out having a meal he just said, "I want to live with you and share my life with you. Shall we live together? What do you think?"

"Yes, I would like that," I said, my mind racing and my heart beating fast.

It was all so scary. I was happy with my house-mates but I wanted a life with Bill. It all frightened me.

What if I make a mistake?

"I understand your hesitation, but I am going to have

my own flat tomorrow. Maybe you can come and stay over now and again in the beginning and we can see how it goes," he quickly said.

"Yes, that would be a good idea," I replied with a sigh of relief.

Bill understood my hesitation. He got the flat and I went to look at it. It was in Wath-upon-Dearne and it was in a good area. It was the upper floor of a Victorian semi-detached. So, it was quite spacious and had two big bedrooms. It was furnished so he had moved in straight away.

"It's a lovely flat, Bill," I said.

"Yes, I chose it with you in mind," he replied. I didn't say a word. "Maybe you will stop over sometime," he quickly said.

"Yes, I will, but don't rush me," I replied.

"I won't," he said. We spent the evening at the flat. Bill cooked a meal and afterwards we watched the television. It felt nice and cosy.

"Well, let's take you home, Patricia," he said getting up. I felt sad to leave but I knew I had to go.

"Okay," I said as I stood up. We got back to my place about 11 p.m. He kissed me and said, "See you tomorrow and I will phone you during the day,"

"Okay," I said getting out of the car and going into the house. I do miss him when I'm not with him.

It was about two weeks before I stayed over one night. I was happy but nervous. Bill was such a good host, making sure I was all right and not pushing me for anything. He just wanted me to relax. Over the next few months, I stayed over some nights until I felt comfortable. Then, I moved in. It felt so right at that time.

LOSS OF FAITH

On the day of my move, the lads were sad when I left, and so was I. It was like someone had ripped a piece of my heart out, because they were really like brothers to me. They helped me load my car with all of my things. But it was done in silence.

"We are going to miss you, Patricia," Patrick said as Tony nodded.

"I will miss you both, too," I replied with a croak in my voice. I hated good-byes. "But I will come back and visit you," I quickly said.

"You'd better," Tony replied.

I gave them both a big hug and got in my car saying, "I will. You will see." I dared not look at them as tears were running down my face and there was a big lump in my throat, as I drove away. My heart filled with sadness.

They have been so good to me. Even Mother eventually softened to them, and she did admit that they were nice people.

Bill was not at home when I landed at the flat. I had my own key and unloaded my car. By the time he came home from work, I had put everything away. I had prepared a meal and set the table with candles burning. He came up the stairs and into the living room, his hands behind his back. As he walked towards me, he brought his arm from behind his back and there was a beautiful bunch of red roses.

"These are for you to welcome you to our new home," he said, looking happy. He flung his arms around me and kissed me, still holding the flowers.

"I am happy to be here, too," I replied. I placed the flowers in a vase and put the dinner out. It was a romantic dinner for two in candlelight. I had prepared steak, as Bill loved his steak. After eating, we watched TV and then went to bed. Our first night really together, in our new home.

The days and weeks got better and better, and our relationship was growing.

Bill and I had a loving relationship and he always made me laugh. Everything seemed so perfect.

Is this what I have been waiting for all my life?

Everything felt so good. I was so in love and was having such a good time. It was perfect in my eyes.

My faith was getting stronger. I was reading more and more spiritual books to gain knowledge and attending courses to learn and meet like-minded people. The more I did this, the more I realized that the knowledge was already there, and much more.

I seemed to know far more than I was being taught, and I knew much more than I was reading. It was really strange. The more I read and learned, the more dreams I would have.

Past lives would appear in my dreams and show me where the knowledge had come from. This fascinated me and I had to know more. But patience was a lesson I had to learn, because knowledge comes in its own time, piece by piece.

My happiness had accelerated my spiritual growth and I liked that. I could cope with it much better when I was happy and I was more open to new things.

One day Bill came home and said. "I have been offered a job in Newcastle. Would you like move there? I know you have a good job so think about it. We don't have to go if you don't want to."

"Okay, I will give it some thought," I replied.

For the first time, it was not an 'either – or' situation. I did not have to give something up. I had a choice and that felt good.

I decided to go to my boss and have a discussion with him. I sat down on the spare chair in his office, which I noticed was always spick and span. Everything had its place, in tidy piles.

"You wanted to see me, Patricia," he said, looking up at me.

"Yes. Bill has been offered a job in Newcastle and he has asked if I want to go with him," I replied nervously.

"That's funny, I was already thinking of sending you to the Newcastle factories. They need sorting out and your expertise is required. So, I will move things forward, so you can go at the same time as your partner. It will be for about two years and that will give you a chance to sort out what you are doing and what you want to do in the longer term. I don't want to lose you, Patricia," he said.

"Thank you. I will inform Bill," I quickly replied as I left his office. Everything was falling into place. I just could not believe it. I was filled with excitement. A new home, and new job as I had seen in my dreams.

I was late coming home that night as work had been busy. Bill had cooked a meal and was just putting it out as I walked in. I had a big smile on my face.

"You are beaming like a Cheshire cat," he quickly said.

"Yes, I am," I replied laughing.

"Well, what's it all about?" he said.

LOSS OF FAITH

"I spoke to my boss about going to Newcastle today and he said he was already thinking about sending me there, so he will bring his plans forward for me so we can go together. We can go to Newcastle," I replied, all excited.

"That's great news. I will talk to my mother and father about staying with them while we get a house," he said excitedly.

"That's great, we can start packing," I said, getting up to wash the pots.

Bill had to serve his notice at work so in the meantime, he sorted out the plans to go to Newcastle. We had to stay with his parents, who were lovely, so that would not be a hardship until we could sort out a place of our own.

A month later we were packing the car up with our clothes and heading for Newcastle.

His parents were welcoming and had made space for us. The weekend went quickly and we both started work on Monday. The Newcastle accent for me was difficult to understand and I kept asking people to repeat slowly what they had said.

We stayed at Bill's parents' house for about four months until we found a flat and bought it. It was in Blythe, Northumberland. The flat was only a ten minute drive from the sea, as well as being surrounded by beautiful countryside. Four months with his parents was just the time it took to purchase the flat. We enjoyed shopping for our furniture, and in between shopping, Bill showed me some of the amazing places around—small fishing ports and old towns and villages. They were beautiful, just as though someone had painted them on a canvass.

We got the keys to our new home and had all our

LOSS OF FAITH

furniture and things delivered. We worked all weekend getting it straight before we had to go to work on Monday. Our new home was finally set up. The people in Newcastle were very friendly and in the short time we had been there, we had made lots of good friends.

One night after we had moved in, we were having our meal and Bill said, looking at me, "Will you marry me?"

"Yes, I will," I replied. So he put his hand in his pocket, pulling out a small ring box, and gave it to me. "This is for you," he said.

I opened it, all excited. It was a beautiful Ruby and diamond ring set in yellow gold. "It's beautiful!" I replied, putting it on my finger. "How did you know my size?" I asked.

"Oh, I have been sneaking your rings out of the house to the jewellers to make sure I got it right," he replied. "So, we are engaged now," he said.

"Yes, we are," I replied.

"We will plan the wedding then," he said.

"Yes, just a quiet one with a few friends and your family," I replied.

"If that's what you want, that's how it will be," he said.

The next weekend, I went with friends to choose my outfit and hat. A pale green flowery, floaty outfit, and a big hat. Because of the distance, my family couldn't make it to the wedding, which was disappointing, but I understood. So we had just friends and his family on the day. It was a lovely warm, sunny, summer's day and our ceremony was in Morpeth Registry office. It was a good day and we par-

LOSS OF FAITH

tied into the early hours of the morning as everyone came back to our flat. When they had left we just collapsed into bed, we were exhausted.

In Newcastle everyone certainly knows how to enjoy themselves. We were engaged and married within three months. But, we had lived together for about twelve months first, so there did not seem to be anything out of the ordinary.

Bill was romantic and we visited all the romantic places in Northumberland and Scotland. Everything was so unbelievable, and I was so happy.

I changed my name on all my documents to my married name, and we opened a joint bank account, as married couples do. Both of our salaries were deposited into that account.

He was the perfect husband with the perfect parents. They were so good to me. This was like a dream come true to me. I was so happy.

Even my daughter came for a holiday to Newcastle and spent a long weekend, because her grandparents had contacted me. Unfortunately, they were having problems with her and just really wanted a break to see if I could sort her out. There was nothing wrong. She was growing up and had opinions of her own.

We had a good time together and I took her places. Bill was very good with her, so that helped. He really did make an effort to make her feel welcome. He made her laugh and played silly games with her. It felt very much like she was his daughter.

What more could I want?

Bill wanted children, so we were trying to have a

LOSS OF FAITH

child, but nothing was happening. The more you want it the less it happens.

It just is not the right time.

Everything was simply perfect. We had our own home, were both working, had goods friends, and we were in love and enjoying life.

❋ ★ ❋

Chapter Thirty-Four

Ultimate Deception

We had been married for about six weeks when I kept getting a bad feeling that something was about to happen, but I could not see what. I kept questioning this, as everything was so good.

Am I just being paranoid because I was so happy? Are they just my own fears?

I kept remembering what the Angel had said, "Enjoy what you have for whatever time it lasts." Things were just rushing into my head. I just couldn't stop it.

So, I kept trying to push these feelings to the back of my mind. Romantic happiness had eluded me before meeting Bill, and I just did not want to do anything to spoil it.

But this feeling of something bad about to happen would not go away no matter how much I pushed it to the back of my mind.

What could it be, when I am so happy? Who is playing with my mind? Am I just going mad?

LOSS OF FAITH

About two days later, I woke up with a real bad feeling that something was going to happen that day.

Nothing was different. Bill got up and gave me a big hug and kiss as he always did, and off he went to work as usual, and I left for work a short while later.

All day at work, I felt bad and had a feeling of loss, so much so, that I felt sick inside. I phoned Bill about lunch time.

"Hi honey, is everything all right?" he asked.

"Everything is fine, just wanted to say Hi as I have been busy with work," I quickly replied. "See you tonight," I quickly said and hung up the phone.

He seemed all right and his normal self. This feeling was driving me mad, so I phoned home and Father answered.

"Hi, Father, is everyone okay at your end?" I asked, trying not to let him hear the nervousness in my voice.

"Yes, we are all fine," he replied What's wrong?" he replied in a questioning voice.

"Oh, nothing is wrong. I hadn't had chance to phone you lately as work has been busy. So I thought I would give you a quick call from work that's all," I quickly replied.

"Are you sure, Patricia?" he said in a worried tone.

"Yes, Father, everything is fine. Have to go as work is busy, so I'll ring you over the weekend," I said rushing the words out before he asked me any more questions. "Bye Father, I love you," I said putting the phone down.

I knew my father was sensing something was wrong as he knows me well, but I just couldn't explain my bad feelings. At least all my family was all right so that ruled

LOSS OF FAITH

that one out. That left only Bill, but nothing seemed wrong. I had spoken to him and everything seemed okay. It was just this bad feeling that would not go away.

I must be going mad.

I decided it must be me and just buried my head in my work, trying to put it to the back of my mind.

I left work about 5:30 p.m. and headed for home, along the coast road. It was beautiful and peaceful driving along the road with the sea on my left, the sun shining and glistening its light across the water. The sea had a calm stillness, just little tiny waves throwing a white froth on the sandy beach, shimmering in the sun's glow.

It must be me, as nothing has happened. Maybe I am losing it?

When I got home, I started preparing a meal.

Bill phoned, "Hi, honey, I am going to be home late from work so I will sort myself out with food. Not sure what time I will get back. So, see you later."

"Okay, see you later," I replied putting the phone down.

See? Nothing is wrong.

So, I had my dinner and a bath, and then sat watching television as I waited for Bill to come home.

This bad feeling was still there, it just would not go away. It was beginning to drive me mad.

I just wish these thoughts would stop. Go away!

I fell asleep watching the television and when I woke up it was midnight and no sign of Bill. My heart sank. I tried phoning, but no response.

Oh, maybe he is out with his work colleagues and you're over-reacting. He sometimes does this, you know that.

LOSS OF FAITH

So, I decided to go to bed and try and get some sleep. I kept telling myself that everything was all right. I tossed and turned, snatching fifteen minutes of sleep here and there, but was still not able to settle down.

I just kept watching the clock go round and round and still no sign of Bill. By 6:00 a.m., I was distraught and got up. I just did not know what was happening.

Where is Bill? Has something happened to him?

I tried phoning him, but no answer. My heart was pounding and my head was all over the place. I was shaking like a leaf.

This is not like him at all.

I started ringing all the hospitals in panic, thinking he may have had an accident, or had fallen ill. But, there was nothing. I phoned his work only to find that he had left work on time yesterday and not turned in today.

I phoned all of our friends but no one had seen him. There was no way I could go to work, so I phoned in sick. I had to stay home, in case the phone rang and it was Bill or some other person letting me know where he was and what had happened to him.

I could not eat anything, I felt so sick inside and I could not stop crying. I tried racking my brain as to what could have happened. I was such a wreck. The man I loved was not there and I did not know what had happened to him.

About 7:00 p.m. that evening the phone rang. My heart was pounding as I rushed to pick it up. There was this man I did not know on the phone

"Is Bill there?" he said in a stern voice.

"No, he is not. I don't know where he is. Who is this?" I asked in panic, my voice quivering and my body shaking with fear.

He didn't answer. Just a deadly silence on the other end of the phone and then he hung up. It was scary and I was frightened, shaking like a leaf.

What's this all about?

There was a knock at the door, so I went to answer it, still shaking all over, not knowing who it would be.

I shouted, "Who is it?"

"It's Maggie, Patricia," came the reply. I quickly opened the door and let her in, bursting into tears.

"What's wrong, Bill not home yet?" she asked putting her arms around me and giving me a hug.

"No, he is not and I have just had this horrible phone call asking me if he is here and not giving a name, and saying nothing and hanging up," I replied, blurting and bumbling my words in between sobs.

"I am here and staying. I'll make us a cup of tea," she replied sitting me down and putting the kettle on. We drank the tea and sat in the living room.

"I can't understand Bill's absence and where he might be. This is not like him and you two are so much in love. You are the perfect couple. Something must have happened to him. We'll get to the bottom of this. I am sure he will contact you soon," she said.

"I hope so, I miss him and I am really worried," I replied, still shaking with fear. "I am glad you have come round, I really am in a mess," I said in a shaky voice.

"I wouldn't leave you with all this to deal with on your own, Patricia, we are friends," she quickly replied.

While we were talking, the phone rang and Maggie jumped up, "I will answer it," she said, picking up the phone.

"Hello, Maggie speaking," she said in a calm voice. She pulled the phone away from her ear, looked at it saying, "They didn't say anything. They just hung up," as she put the phone back on its hook and sat down again. "That was strange, maybe a sales call," she said.

Could it be Bill?

Just after the call, there was a knock at the door.

"You stay there, Patricia. I will answer it," Maggie said, getting up and going to the front door and opening it. I could hear raised voices. Maggie was really shouting. My heart was racing so fast I could hardly breathe and my body was frozen in the chair. I just couldn't move. Suddenly, three men forced their way past Maggie and into my flat, they came barging into the living room, very angry.

"Where is Bill, we are looking for him," the big fat, bald one said. He was rough looking wearing tatty jeans and a T Shirt, unshaven and mean looking.

"I don't know, he hasn't been home," I replied, my voice shaking with fear and tears rolling down my face.

"Leave her alone," Maggie said.

"Oh, shut up!" the fat one said, grabbing hold of Maggie's arm and flinging her like a rag doll on the settee. The fat one came up to me and put his face in my face and grabbed my arm so tight, saying in a mean and nasty voice,"If you are not telling us the truth, lady, we will be back and if we have to come back there won't be much of your pretty face left to look at. Do you get my meaning?" and flung me onto the floor. Two tall men—dirty, rough looking and unshaven—just stood in the doorway not say-

LOSS OF FAITH

ing a word..

"Yes, I understand. But I don't know where he is," I replied shaking.

"Let's look around the flat," the fat one said, pushing the other two out of the way. They followed him like sheep.

At that moment a sense of courage and determination came over me, as I pushed myself up and ran to the phone, picked it up and dialled 999 for the police. Someone answered saying, "Hello, police emergency service."

I blurted out hurriedly, "Come quickly three men have forced their way into my flat," as I blurted out the address, the three men led by the fat one came running back to the living room.

"It's the police, they are on their way," I screamed, looking straight into the fat one's eyes.

The fat one was about to come forward but the other two panicked and pulled his arm saying, "Come on the police will be here in a minute."

The fat one looked mean and nasty, screwing his face up and holding his fist up to me as the other two pulled him back. They all turned and ran out of the flat. The phone was still off the hook as I ran to the window, seeing an old blue Ford Escort pull away at high speed, screeching it's tyres as it left. By the time I turned round, Maggie was talking to the police saying they had just left and put the phone down.

"You were courageous. What was that all about?" Maggie said, as she grabbed hold of me and gave me a hug. I broke down crying and shaking and Maggie sat me on the settee and remained by my side.

LOSS OF FAITH

"I don't know Maggie. It's all about Bill, but I don't know what or why, I wish I did," I cried, sobbing my heart out, my head on her shoulder. We were both shaken up by the experience, but I know Maggie was holding it together for me. We sat in silence as we could hear the police sirens coming up the road with the blue lights flashing, the car screeching to a halt, the sound of people running up the steps to the flat. Then a knock at the door. My heart sighed with relief.

"I'll let them in, Patricia," Maggie said getting up and answering the door. In walked a male and a female police officer, both very tall, dressed in their uniforms.

"Please sit down," I said still shaking.

"Can you tell us what has happened?" the male officer said.

"Yes," I replied. I went through everything regarding Bill's disappearance the day before, the funny phone call and then the three men. I gave them full descriptions of the men and the car they left in. Maggie backed up my story.

The policeman took all the details, but before he left, he said, "Do you have a joint bank account?"

"Yes. Why?" I asked.

"Have you checked your bank account?" he asked.

"No, but Bill would not do anything. He is a good man," I said, puzzled.

"Go and check it tomorrow, just in case. At least, if everything is all right, then your mind will be at rest," he said.

"Okay, I will go and check our bank account," I replied.

Then, he left, saying he would be in touch.

"I wonder what he meant by that?" Maggie said.

LOSS OF FAITH

"I don't know, but I will check tomorrow," I replied.

"I am going to stay the night," Maggie said.

"Thanks, Maggie, I just don't want to be on my own, the spare room is made up," I replied.

We sat quietly watching TV, but the phone kept ringing. We would take turns to answer it, but no one spoke and they just kept hanging up. We both kept shaking our heads. It was unnerving and caused me anxiety.

It is a good thing Maggie is staying, otherwise I would be very frightened.

The phone stopped ringing about midnight, so we went to bed. I couldn't sleep.

What was this all about and where is Bill?

Everything was just going through my head.

I was frightened and so sad. I just stared out the window at the full moon in a clear sky, the stars so clear and bright. I kept crying and every bit of my body hurt. I watched the dawn break and heard the birds doing their morning calls. I was physically and mentally exhausted. As dawn broke, I got up and made a cup of tea. I could not go to work as I was a real mess. Maggie finally got up at about 8 a.m. and I made her a cup of tea.

"I am going to the bank with you today, Patricia. You're not going alone. I will phone work and get the day off," she said.

"Thanks, Maggie, you are a good friend. I appreciate it," I replied.

We both phoned our work and headed for the bank in Maggie's car, as I was not fit to drive.

We walked into the bank and waited in the queue.

When it was my turn, I asked, "Can I see my balance,

please?"

"Oh, we can't show you," the girl said.

"What do you mean you can't show me?" I replied, agitated.

"I can't show you. You will have to see the bank manager, so will you please take a seat," she said, going off into the bank manager's office.

Maggie and I went to sit down.

"This is very strange," I said looking at Maggie.

"It is, but it will be all right," she replied.

Suddenly, the girl came walking across to us and said, "Can you follow me to the manager's office, please?"

We got up and followed her into this clinical looking meeting room at the back, where this smartly dressed man in his forties sat behind the desk. "Please, come in and take a seat," he said without smiling. We sat down and he said, "What's the problem?"

This seemed strange because he had my file in front of him and he certainly had read it. The papers were not neatly placed.

I explained what had happened and that the policeman had suggested that I come to the bank and have a look at the account.

The bank manager listened and when I had finished, he sat quietly.

"Can I see the bank statement, please?" I asked.

The manager sat quietly, rubbing his chin.

"I need to know where I am with money, so can you either show me the statement or tell me what is in our account," I asked, anxiously.

By this time, I was in panic mode with a terrible feel-

LOSS OF FAITH

ing inside.

"I don't need to show the statement. Your account is overdrawn," he said.

"What?" I cried.

"Patricia, the account is overdrawn. All the money is gone. The £10,000 and the £200 approved overdraft has been used, and the account is £500 overdrawn above the approved overdraft and checks are bouncing on the account every day. All we can do is freeze the account for now and set you up with another account. You do realize though, that you are responsible for the account, if he can't be found. But, we can work something out. You have been a good customer. Let's get some documents completed so you are all right, and you can get your wages paid into another account," he said.

I was stunned and in shock. My friend put her arm around me and I burst into tears.

"How could he do this to me? He seemed so nice and loving and all he wanted was the money. I feel so foolish and now I have to get myself out of this mess," I cried.

"You will get yourself out of this. I was fooled by him as well. He seemed so nice," Maggie replied.

I could not stop shaking. My heart was broken and I felt so much pain.

What a fool I have been to trust and give my heart openly, only to get hurt. Why did you not show me this before now? Why did you let me love him? I hate God and I never want to have anything to do with God ever again. I have been misled by God into believing I had real love and a good man. I had a glimpse of happiness and then, it was taken away. I cannot trust anymore in God.

LOSS OF FAITH

I left the bank in complete shock in total disbelief at what I had been told.

How could anyone do this to anyone, let alone to someone they said they loved? Not even thinking about what mess they are leaving you in or how you will survive. I will never love anyone again.

I could not speak and we drove home in silence.

We got back to my place and Maggie said, "I will stay here with you for a while until you decide what you are doing."

"Thanks, I just don't want to be on my own," I cried.

She was just as shocked as I was. I could only stare at the wall while Maggie sat in silence watching TV.

I just can't believe what has happen. I just feel so foolish. I can't talk to Father yet!

At 9 p.m. Maggie and I had a cup of tea and we went to bed. The events of the last few days had exhausted us both. Maggie understood my silence but she wanted to be there for me.

I couldn't sleep. I kept crying until there were no more tears to shed and eventually I dropped to sleep.

Chapter Thirty-Five

On My Own Again!

Over the next couple of days, Maggie stayed with me, going to work and coming back at night to the flat. I couldn't go to work as I could not stop crying and I could not eat. I had phoned my boss to keep him in the picture and he was very understanding. I felt so foolish and had so much hurt inside. There was no communication from Bill, which hurt even more, as he did not care what he had done to me.

What a fool I have been. I have failed at yet another relationship.

On Wednesday, the policeman and policewoman came to see me.

"We wanted to keep you informed of the situation," the policewoman said. "Bill has left the country and he had not just taken your money. We have received complaints from his friends and other people that he has taken money from them as well, for a business deal, where nothing has happened. He is a con man, and he also has a previous criminal record and has been to prison," the policeman said.

"What, this is not the man I married," I replied bursting into tears.

"Are you sure we are talking about the same Bill, as he is a lovely man," Maggie quickly asked.

"Yes, we have got the right Bill. He is good at what he does. Everyone who has loaned him money for a business deal has been trying to get in touch with him. When they couldn't, they called the police. Bill has obtained money by deception from many people and when we catch him, which we will, he will be prosecuted," the policeman said.

I burst into tears saying, "I feel so foolish, how could I have not seen it?"

Maggie put her arm around me to comfort me. "That explains all the phone calls and the three men turning up at the flat," Maggie said, as though a light bulb had gone off in her head.

My mind was all over the place. I felt dizzy with a pressure in my head at the same time. My body was in panic. I was shaking all over and trembling with a cold feeling, just like icicles creeping up my whole body.

"Try not to feel foolish, because this man is very good at what he does. He has been to prison before for the same thing. He just needed you for a front. You are a lovely person, and being married to you gave him credibility with other people. He will go to prison again, but for longer this time," the policeman said getting up. "Let me know if he does contact you and if you are going away at all, let me know where you are going," he said.

LOSS OF FAITH

"I will," I replied.

"Will you be staying with Patricia, Maggie? I don't think she should be left alone just now. Only because of health reasons," the police woman said.

"I am not going anywhere, I will be here while she needs me," Maggie quickly said.

She really is my Angel and my strength.

Maggie got up to show them both out and came back into the living room, sitting down beside me.

"I can't believe all this. Bill has fooled us all," Maggie said in disbelief.

"I know, I can't believe it either. I feel so foolish," I replied, sobbing and shaking at the same time.

"No need to feel foolish. He fooled everyone," Maggie replied.

I know the policeman was trying to be helpful, but I was having mixed emotions: being happy he would go to prison and feeling sadness for him at the same time.

But, I could not forgive him. It was such a traumatic time. I could not work for the next few weeks and Maggie stayed with me, which was a relief.

During this time, all of our friends started to phone me, because Bill had taken their money, and they had been told that I had been taken for a ride as well.

They apologized to me for not contacting me sooner, and for thinking I had anything to do with it. It did hurt me that they would even think that I would be involved in such a thing.

Did people really think I could do this?

So, Bill had not just taken my money, he had caused people to think badly of me, until I was proven innocent.

LOSS OF FAITH

Our friends started to come to see me, but how could things be the same? They made sure that I had company and took me out, but I was in 'robot' mode—not really wanting to go out and just going through the motions.

I had to think about my future and what I wanted to do and where I wanted to be. Work was all I had, so I had to sort that out.

After a time, I was feeling a little stronger so I phoned Father.

"Hello, Father. I am in trouble. Bill has disappeared and cleared out our bank account and used the overdraft, and kept bouncing checks on the account and left me in debt, which I have to sort out. The police are involved as he has taken money from friends on the pretense of a business deal. They haven't found him yet, but he has already done this before and has been to prison for it, the police told me. I feel so foolish," I explained, crying as I told my story.

"Don't feel foolish, Patricia. You have a good heart and he is a con man. Come home Patricia," he said in a worried voice.

"I will Father, I just need to sort out work first, and I can put the flat on the market and leave the keys with the estate agent. I will let you know when, but I am hoping in about a month," I replied, sobbing my heart out.

"Phone me everyday, Patricia. Will you do that for me? You are such a long way away and I want to know you are all right. I have had a feeling for weeks," he replied anxiously.

"I will Father. Speak to you tomorrow," I said, putting the phone down.

LOSS OF FAITH

I then phoned my boss back in Yorkshire and explained what had happened.

"I am sorry to hear that, Patricia. You have done an excellent job in Newcastle and everything is working there now. So your time in there is coming to an end and I need you back in Yorkshire," he said in a strong, positive voice.

"That's amazing," I replied with a sigh of relief. "I think one month should clear up Newcastle and you can come back to the Yorkshire factory after that, and we will sort things out from there. What do you think, Patricia?" he asked.

"That would be about right," I replied.

"Okay then, you work around that time frame and I'll see you when you get back," he said.

"Great, see you when I am back," I replied, putting the phone down, my heart feeling lighter, as I could finally go home.

That pleased me in one way, but it meant I was going back to live with my parents, yet again. I had spoken to Father about what had happened and I know he said to come home, but I had to make my own choices. So, thinking things through was important. Now, with work falling into place, I could finally go home.

I had to sort out the flat and put it up with estate agents to sell it. It was in our joint names, so not knowing where Bill was, made it difficult. The estate agents put it up for sale, hoping that Bill would be found. I also had to let the police know where I was going so they could contact me when they found him and let me know what was happening. This was embarrassing, because I felt like a criminal having to report my movements.

LOSS OF FAITH

Maggie had gone back to her flat, as I was holding it together better now and work was keeping me fully occupied.

I started packing and selling things with the help of Maggie and friends, so the flat would be empty when I left. I had to see Bill's parents before I left because they loved me like a daughter and were devastated by what had happened. They thought Bill had learned his lesson the first time. They hoped that meeting me, would have helped him and kept him out of trouble. They were really angry with him and did not want to know their own son anymore.

Everyone was coming out of the woodwork to help me pack and sort things out. They were all sad I was leaving, but understood why.

Bill had affected all our lives and caused so much pain and unhappiness, especially for his parents. I felt so sorry for them. His father had Parkinson's disease, and all this upset had made him even worse. They did not want to lose contact with me, and said I could stay with them anytime I wanted.

Where is God in all this? Bill's parents did not deserve this, and neither did I. If ever there was a God, He certainly was not around at this time. Bill was so selfish.

For me, God did not exist, and I was questioning everything, again.

The day I left the flat, I felt that I was closing down a chapter in my life, which included happiness and sadness.

Where will my life take me next? I only have my work now.

When I left, I never looked back. My memories were too painful to look at the flat for one last time. Tears were streaming down my face.

LOSS OF FAITH

I am back to square one, starting again, back at my parents' house. When will all this end and when will I be truly happy?

The journey home seemed long and slow. I wanted to get there, but at the same time, I did not want to get there. Every time I returned home, I felt like I had failed.

I got to my parents' house about 4:00 p.m., just in time for tea. Father was so happy to see me. He threw his arms around me and hugged me saying, " I am so pleased you are home, so I can see you, and help you. I did not like your being in the flat in Newcastle on your own."

"I am glad to be home too, Father. I had lots of friends helping me and it was sad to leave them, but I know I needed to be home," I replied, crying. I looked at Mother, who was non-committal, which meant that Father had had a word with her. She said nothing as usual, but her body language said everything, as she sat at the kitchen table with her arms folded and a stern look on her face. Her eyes were not filled with love, but anger.

I did not feel much like talking, but Father was trying to cheer me up by asking about my journey home and the job I was taking on now. Mother just listened.

After tea, Father helped me unload the car and get everything to my bedroom. I unpacked and then lay down on the bed to get some sleep, as it had been a tiring and emotional journey home.

I did not realize how tired I was, and I slept until 10:00 a.m. the next morning. I was awakened by Father's bringing me a cup of tea to bed. I knew he could feel my pain and was trying to cheer me up. He was worried about me because I had lost so much weight and was not eating properly.

LOSS OF FAITH

"How are you this morning, Patricia?" he asked.

"I am okay, Father. I will get up in a minute. I am just so tired. This has taken so much out of me," I replied.

"I know but you are home and safe now with us and we can look after you until you get back on your feet," he said, as he left the bedroom.

That brought tears to my eyes. I sat up in bed drinking my tea and crying. I felt so alone, but I knew I was in good hands with my father. He was such a lovely man.

I got washed and dressed and went downstairs. Mother and Father were sitting in the lounge. I knew they had been talking about me as I could hear the conversation upstairs and as soon as I walked in the room, Mother went quiet. Father was worried about me and wanted Mother to give me an easier time than she usually did.

"Do you want some breakfast?" Mother asked.

"No, thanks. I will just have a cup of tea," I replied.

"You have to eat something," she said.

"Mother, I don't want to eat. I just want a cup of tea," I said, walking off into the kitchen.

I heard Father say, "Leave her alone. She will eat when she is ready."

I just could not face food. My stomach would not take it. All I was doing was drinking tea.

I know Father was worried as the weight was just dropping off me. In two months, I had lost about two stone in weight and I was beginning to look too thin and my face was drawn. But, right now, I just could not eat.

All this had left me with so many unanswered questions.

Did Bill ever really love me? How could he have been so loving and caring and do this? We had lived together

LOSS OF FAITH

for well over a year. Why wait until we got married? Why would he do this to his friends? How could he hurt his parents this way? Was this just all about money? Did he like me at all?

I just could not stop thinking. Everything had left me feeling empty and hurt. I feared I would never get my answers.

How can my heart heal from this when so many questions are unanswered? How can I ever trust anyone again? Here I am again, back home and on my own again.

Chapter Thirty-Six

Facing My Demons

I was glad to be back at work on Monday because I needed to put my head into something to get me on track and focused.

While I was at work on the first day, I was holding back the tears. I was such a fool. I could not explain to anyone how I really felt. I could feel myself going down and down as the day progressed, and I was so glad to see the end of the day. No one could tell that anything was wrong with me. At work, I was used to showing only the professional Patricia, but inside, I was all mixed up with my emotions.

When I left work, I said goodnight to everyone and felt that I was not going to see them again. I got into my car and set off for home, feeling very sad. As I was driving, that feeling of sadness turned into a feeling of not wanting to live. It became so strong, that all I could see was this tree in front of me and my car was headed straight for it. It

LOSS OF FAITH

was all in slow motion. All I could feel was this numbness inside and I could see a white light in front of me. It was like being in a hypnotic state.

As I was heading for the tree, out of the white light came an angel. She grabbed the steering wheel of the car and turned it away from the tree. My feet were pushed off the accelerator pedal and someone else hit the brakes and the car came screeching to a halt.

I burst into tears and cried out, "I don't want to live anymore!"

"It's not your time, Patricia," a voice said.

"I have heard all this before and I just can't take anymore. Just go away and leave me alone," I cried.

Then, the voice said, "You have a lot to do in your life, Patricia, and lots of people to help."

When I heard those words, this great sense of peace came over me, and I just sat in the car crying my eyes out until there were no tears left to shed. I felt a weight had been lifted from my body and that I could really get on with my life.

I started to drive and pulled over at a petrol station to wash my face and put my makeup back on, so I could go home without getting too many questions.

"Are you all right?" the petrol pump attendant asked.

"Yes, I am fine," I replied.

I drove home and walked into the house.

"You're late today," Mother said.

"Yes, I had things to do at work," I replied.

Father looked at me with a sense of knowing, but said nothing.

When Mother went upstairs to get a bath, Father

asked, "Are you all right now, Patricia? I really felt what you were going through earlier."

"Yes, Father, I am fine now. Everything had to come out and it has now, so you don't have to worry. I am fine. I can cope. It won't happen again," I replied.

"That's good, so we won't talk about it again," he said.

I went to bed that night and slept like a log. I was dead to the world, so much so, that Mother had to wake me for work the next morning.

Over the next two weeks, I was beginning to feel a bit like my normal self. One night the phone rang and I answered it.

"Is that, Patricia?" a male voice said.

"Yes, it is," I replied, puzzled.

"It's the police. We just wanted you to know that Bill is back in the UK and has given himself up."

"That's a relief." I replied.

"There is just one thing, he is out on bail and living in Goldthorpe" he said.

My heart sank and I couldn't speak. Goldthorpe was the next village to where my parents lived.

"Are you there, Patricia?" the policeman asked.

"Oh, oh, yes. That's a shock though. Bill living so close to me. I thought he would be in Newcastle," I quickly said.

"Goldthorpe is where he wanted to be and we could not stop that. This is his new address so you can give it to your solicitor. If he bothers you, let us know and we will do something about it," he replied.

"I will, thank you," I replied quickly, writing the address down and slowly putting the phone down.

LOSS OF FAITH

Panic started to set in.

Why has he come here, instead of Newcastle?

I now had his address to get things sorted out for the divorce papers and the estate agents. That was my main concern, before he decided to disappear again.

"So, he is living in Goldthorpe?" Father asked.

"Yes, Father, he has given himself up and is out on bail living there. Fantastic," I said sarcastically. I definitely was not happy that he was living so close.

"You didn't expect him to stay in Newcastle after what he did there," Father said. He always spoke sense.

"I don't suppose so, Father, but he could have gone anywhere but Goldthorpe," I replied angrily.

All this was doing my head in and bringing back all those bad memories and feelings. I was so angry with Bill.

"I just can't talk about it Father, so I am going to bed," I said getting up and heading for the stairs door.

"Okay, Patricia, Goodnight" Father said.

"Goodnight," I replied, heading upstairs to bed.

It's funny Mother is keeping well out of things these days. Whatever Father has said, it's working.

I just could not feel any love from my Mother, so I kept quiet and to myself as far as she was concerned.

I got up the next day and went to work. I made phone calls to my solicitor and the estate agents to get things moving. I did not want to see Bill because I hated him for what he had done to me, and the others. But being so close, there was a good chance that I could bump into him, so I needed to avoid Goldthorpe at all costs.

My day at work was busy and I was tired when I got home. I had eaten at work so I went into the living room

LOSS OF FAITH

and sat watching TV as my head was spinning like a top, and I really didn't want to talk to Mother. So far, the only contribution Mother had made to all this was that he must still have feelings for me.

I don't care whether he has or not. There is no chance of us getting back together because I am filing for divorce and he should get the papers this week.

Father has told Mother to leave me alone to make my own choices. I know she was trying to be helpful.

I still had feelings for Bill, but my heart was broken and I had lost all trust in him. There was no way I would make up with him after everything he had done.

Mother must be crazy to think that I ever would.

After tea, my parents joined me in the living room and watched TV. Not a great deal was said. It was just small talk. Everyone felt awkward. It was better to say nothing than to put their foot in things.

My life had become, yet again, all work and no play. I was having nothing to do with God or anything else. Father tried talking to me about faith and trust, but I was not having any of it, so after awhile, he gave up and allowed me the space to find my own way.

Over the next two weeks, I went to work and stayed late because I did not want to go home.

My car was coming up for service, so I booked it into the garage for the next day. I could drop it in the morning, walk to work, and pick it up in the evening, after I had finished. The garage was just round the corner from work, which was convenient.

I got up early the next day and dropping my car off was my first priority. I had forgotten my lunch, so I quick-

LOSS OF FAITH

ly went to the shop to get something. As I came out of the shop, Bill was standing, looking in the window.

I had to look twice at him because he did not look like his normal self. He looked down and out and was not taking care of himself.

He looked round at me as I came out of the doorway.

"Hello, Patricia," he said.

"Hello, are you following me?" I asked, my heart beating fast. I felt all sorts of emotions, from anger, sadness, frustration. I just wanted to hit him, but I didn't. I held back the tears.

"I saw you and wanted to talk to you," he said, with a sad look.

"I don't think there is much to say, after what you have done, do you?" I replied, in anger. My pulse was racing and I was feeling panic setting in.

"Can we go and have a cup of tea?" he enquired.

"Not now, as I have to go to work. I have to pick up my car at six this evening. We can meet then at the café," I replied, walking off. I had to leave as my emotions were all over the place and I needed to keep them under control. I knew this would happen one day, but I just did not expect it now.

I needed to get to work and put some time and space between us to get my head straight. I felt sorry for him but he had caught me by surprise. I needed to be in the right frame of mind to meet him, if I was going to meet him at all, and that was my question.

All day long, one question went through my head. *Will I, or won't I meet him?* I really could not make up my mind.

LOSS OF FAITH

It was nearly 6:00 p.m. and I left work to pick up the car. I drove and parked the car near the café for about five minutes, debating on whether I should meet up with him or not. Suddenly, I decided to go and face my demons. I landed at the café about ten past six and Bill was sitting there waiting.

I walked up to him, sat down at the table and ordered tea.

"I did not think you were coming," Bill said.

"I nearly didn't but then thought we had things to talk about and sort out," I replied.

"Yes, the divorce and the flat," he said.

"Yes," I replied.

"Do you want the divorce?" Bill asked.

"Yes, I do. You have hurt me, taken my money and left me in debt. What did you expect from me? I can't trust you. You probably never loved me and just used me," I said calmly.

"Well, I do love you. I don't know why I did it. I have now to pay the penalty for what I have done. I won't fight the divorce or selling the flat, if that is what you want. I don't, but I understand why you want to do it. I just wanted to say I am so sorry. I will do whatever you want me to. I know I have lost you and I am sad about that because you are such a special person. This is all my fault," he said.

"Well, it changes nothing, Bill. I want nothing more to do with you and I want to get divorced and sell the flat. That way, all ties are broken with you. I can say no more. So, I am going to go home now," I said putting some money on the table to pay the bill. I got up and left, without looking back.

LOSS OF FAITH

My feelings and emotions were through the roof. I still loved Bill but there was no future in it because I would never be able to trust him, ever again. How he looked now was up to him. I did not hold the key to that. He did. He was responsible for his actions then—and now. But, it did not stop me feeling sorry for him because I still loved him. My life had to move on because I could never believe that he ever loved me because of what he had done.

Life is not easy and I had to make choices for myself and nobody else.

I spent several restless days not being able to eat or sleep properly. All I could think about, and see, was Bill. Remembering what he was, to what he is now.

I told my parents that I had seen Bill, so, nobody was questioning me. They gave me the space I needed to sort myself out.

About three days later, I got home from work and Father said, "I bumped into Bill today, and he looks in a sorry state. I felt sorry for him. He really has let himself go."

"I know Father, but I am not responsible for him. He is responsible for himself. He caused all this, not me. So he is doing this to himself. What about me in all this, or don't I count?" I asked, in anger.

"Of course you count, above anything else, Patricia," he said.

"He is a con man. How do you know this is not just another act to get sympathy?" I asked.

"You don't know, Patricia," he replied.

"Well, nothing has changed with me. I am still going through with my divorce as planned, and starting all over again," I said.

"Whatever you decide is all right, Patricia," he replied.

"I am going out for a drive and a walk. I need some time to myself," I said, as I left the house.

Yes, I still loved Bill, but there was all the hurt from what he had done, and how he had done it. I would have rather given him the money than have him take it the way he did, leaving me with no answers as to why.

Finding out that he had taken my money, without any sort of explanation, caused me so much hurt and pain. I still had not found all the answers, but I really could not be bothered. I had faced him, which meant that I had faced my own feelings. Now, I could be strong enough to close things down and move on.

These last few days were about getting a perspective on things and dealing with my emotions. I was not angry anymore. Feeling sorry for Bill was about letting go in order to move on. I could now forgive him for what he had done, because I knew it was his loss, not mine.

Someday, I will find someone else who will truly love me.

The walk had done me good. Father pressing my buttons (because he had seen Bill) was also good. It helped me face myself and my feelings and put it all behind me. I could now face the future, whatever it was going to be.

I went back home, walked in, made myself a cup of tea and sat in the kitchen by myself. After about half an hour, Father came in and sat down.

"Well, Patricia, are you all right?" he asked.

"I am fine, Father. I am sorry for the outburst but I had to deal with my emotions. Now, I have had my walk. I

LOSS OF FAITH

have everything in perspective and my decisions are right for me. I am ready to close the door and move on with my life. I have things worked out and I am really fine now," I replied.

"That's all I wanted to hear, Patricia. I want to see you happy within yourself, and not tormented," he said, as he got up and gave me a big hug.

A real sense of relief came over me, as though a part of me had gone and a new part had been installed.

I never did see or hear from Bill again and neither did my father.

My divorce came through. The flat sold and paid some of my debt off, but not all. It took me another twelve months to pay it all off, but I was glad when it was done. That was the final piece of the puzzle that closed the door fully on Bill, and a chapter in my life that I will never forget. But now, I have forgiveness in my heart. I could only do what was right and in my thoughts I thanked him for being a part of my life. I had felt great love and lost it, but I had learned a lot about me.

I heard from the police that Bill had been sentenced to five years in prison for taking money by deception. He had received a lighter sentence for admitting the offences and giving himself up to the police. Maybe, he did love me, and had to feel a sense of loss and guilt for his actions. And maybe, he learned something from me, too.

Chapter Thirty-Seven

In My Element

The next couple of years were about me. I was not looking for a relationship. I just wanted time to find me again. Who was I? I just did not know and that's what I needed to find out. Bill had set all sorts of questions off in my head, and I needed to find some answers for myself before entering another relationship.

Looking back on my life, I found patterns that had emerged. From my relationship with my mother, to being raped, I had done things out of need rather than want. I had attracted abusive men, out of need, whether it was mental, physical or sexual.

Money was also a pattern that was repeating: having it, then not having it, letting things be taken away. There was always a battle over money. Men wanted me for who I was, but when they had me, they were jealous of my work and how much I earned, compared to them. I had given up my singing for men, too, and gave them so much of

LOSS OF FAITH

myself and got very little in return.

I had a lot of jealousy from other women, so I did not have many female friends. I also found that I was very good at running away from things, rather than facing up to them and dealing with them.

What would life hold for me, if I did not work on myself to attract the right things towards me? I had my work which I was good at, but my personal relationships with men were not good.

I had married young and had my daughter when I was only eighteen years old. So, I never really experienced my teenage years as I should have, like going out with the girls and having fun. I had not even been on holiday with friends and let my hair down. So, it was time to do that and find out who I really was.

I decided to take some time out from relationships and focus on myself. I had my full time work (that was going well), and I was getting promotions, but I needed something more.

Friends were few and far between and the ones I did have were married. How could I go out on my own? That was difficult. But I had to overcome this 'all work and no play' lifestyle.

The only way I could see to do that was to get a weekend job behind a bar. That way, I could work, be sociable and meet people. There was a new bar that had opened in Barnsley which was very popular. They had singing and dancing, which was what I loved.

I felt a great desire to get out and meet people and start my life on a different note this time. I wanted to go slowly and find myself again. There was a need to focus on me and try to heal myself from my past experiences, before entering into another relationship.

I really wanted to work on getting rid of the patterns that had emerged in my life, so I did not repeat them. So far, I had experienced disastrous relationships, and I wanted to find out what was within me that was attracting them to me.

I phoned the bar in Barnsley and went in for an interview. They were nice people and happy to take me on. I only wanted to work Saturday and Sunday but they were short staffed, so I agreed to help them out for a while.

They were interested in my singing and wanted me to sing at the bar as well, which was good for me. So, we agreed that I would start the next day, learn the bar work, and then start to do some singing. Everything had happened so quickly, but it seemed right.

When I went home, I told my parents what I was doing and Father said, "It would be good for you to get out, as long as you do not overdo things, and wear yourself out."

"I won't Father, I promise," I replied.

"What? Work behind a bar that is common and tarty? What would the neighbours think?" Mother snapped.

"I don't care Mother what the neighbours think or what you think. I am doing it," I snapped back.

Mother was just about to say something when Father quickly said, "Leave the girl alone, Ada. She needs to get out and be with people her own age."

"There you go taking her side again," she said, as she stormed out of the room.

"Leave your Mother to me, Patricia. I will sort it out,"

LOSS OF FAITH

he said following Mother into the next room. I could hear Father telling her to keep out of things and let me get on with my life. He always knew how to handle Mother.

I did not care what Mother thought because I was doing this for me, and nobody else. Mother could never understand me and why I did things. But, this was really important to me and my future.

The next evening, I arrived at the pub at 7:30 p.m. and was shown everything behind the bar and how it worked. I picked things up easily, so it was not a problem for me. I was nervous and excited at the same time. I was out mixing with people and that was all that mattered to me. It was different work to my normal work and I could relax and be really me.

The bar staff were nice and friendly and helped me out, if I got stuck with anything. In fact, everyone was friendly and made me feel welcomed, including the customers. The music and entertainment was good and the evening passed very quickly. I had enjoyed myself and been with people and found myself laughing again. It felt so good.

After a week of working behind the bar, the owners asked me if I would like to sing, so I agreed. Saturday night came and there I was, one minute working behind the bar, and the next, on stage singing. The audience loved my singing and everyone was talking to me about how good I was, and would I do more? The owners were delighted and wanted to do a regular feature with me singing. Here I was, doing the one thing I loved the most, and having it come to the forefront again. I felt so happy when I was singing and I liked making people happy.

LOSS OF FAITH

Over the next month, I did more singing and the pub became packed every night. I was beginning to get tired of working a full time job and working seven days a week at the pub, so something was going to have to change.

I had a word with the pub owners and we settled on my doing Friday, Saturday and Sunday evenings, although they would have liked for me to stay seven nights.

I had my full time job to consider as well as what I wanted to do to change my life and find myself again. There had to be balance to what I did.

I was having fun, meeting people, getting out and singing. At last, I was letting my hair down and enjoying myself in the process. It felt really good.

This is what I have been missing all these years.

Cutting down my hours at the pub made a better balance in my life. I was doing three half hour slots per night, singing at the pub, and the rest of the time serving behind the bar, and that was a good mix for me. Friday, Saturday and Sunday evenings became very busy and people were coming from all over to hear me sing.

My singing had come back at a time when I needed to change my life. It not only made me happy, but it helped me release emotions from the past. I would often find myself driving home, shedding tears in the car, and then feeling calm afterwards.

My father would give me healing at home to help me, and this gave me passion and determination to deal with my past.

Men were asking me out, but I was not going to go out with anyone until I felt really ready. At the moment, I was enjoying my freedom and my life. So, I used to tell

LOSS OF FAITH

them that I did not go out with anyone from work, so it kept things friendly. I did not want to cause any problems or fall out with anyone.

Men would still try to ask me out and it did do my confidence a world of good. I received lots of attention and flattering comments which I easily put into perspective, rather than thinking there was more to it than there was. So, I was certainly making progress. I felt sixteen years old and alive again. It was a wonderful feeling. I really was catching up on all the teenage years I had missed and was enjoying myself so much. Life was going well and so was work. I had not felt this good for years.

Chapter Thirty-Eight

Question Everything

Father often talked to me about my loss of faith, but I just did not want to know. I had pushed everything away as it only caused me pain. Every time I renewed my faith, things went wrong and I went through more pain. So, why should I renew my faith when I was having the best time in my life and really enjoying myself both at work and in my private life? I was not in a relationship and did not feel I was ready to enter another just yet.

Mother thought differently and kept saying, "You need a man in your life," and Father used to say, "Leave the girl alone."

During this time, I was also seeing my daughter about once a month, and sometimes, once every two weeks. She was growing up and wanted to see me. We kept in touch, and I did not push her into seeing me more, even though I wanted it badly. So, I let things go at her pace and enjoyed what I had.

LOSS OF FAITH

Just now, I had everything in my life that I wanted and I was much more relaxed. I felt at peace with myself.

I had a promotion at work, which meant I did a bit more travelling to different sites and had to represent the company at functions.

I went to a function in Sheffield and, at my table, was a man from an engineering company. We were both on our own and sat next to each other, so we talked and danced together. It made a nice change from being on my own at these functions. We exchanged telephone numbers and said we would keep in touch. It had been a pleasant evening and we appeared to get on.

Two months went by and nothing happened. I was not going to be the one who made contact with him, so I destroyed his telephone number.

About a month after that, I had a phone call from him.

"Hello, Patricia. It's Peter, we went to the business function two months ago. Sorry I have not been in touch, but work has been busy and I have been working away, as well as going on holiday. I wondered if you would like to meet up next weekend."

"Yes, that would be nice, but I sing Friday, Saturday and Sunday evening." I replied, surprised I had heard from him.

"Well, we could meet up on Saturday lunchtime, if that's all right with you. I can meet you at the Civic Hall at 12:30,pm, and we can go from there," he replied.

"Yes, that will be good, as I will be in Sheffield. See you then," I replied putting the phone down.

The week did seem to drag as I kept thinking about lunch and Saturday with Peter. I had given up on him as I hadn't heard from him, so it really was a surprise.

This is my first date since Bill.

Saturday came and I set off for Sheffield early, as I had some shopping to do first before meeting Peter. After shopping, I headed for the Civic Centre and when I arrived, he was already standing outside.

He is punctual.

He smiled at me and I smiled back as I walked up to him.

"I know a good restaurant about five minutes walk away. Shall we go there?" he asked.

"Yes, that's fine by me," I replied walking by his side.

"Sorry, I have not been in touch but with working away and my holiday, I haven't had much time," he said.

"That's okay. I have been busy, too," I replied.

We arrived at the restaurant and he was the perfect gentleman. He opened the door for me and let me walk in first and he followed behind me.

The waiter stepped forward and Peter informed him we had a table booked, so he led us to our table and gave us the menus to look at.

We both ordered steak.

It's strange how we both liked the same things.

We both chatted over lunch mainly about work and he asked about my singing. Time passed quickly, and I had to get home to get ready for my evening job.

"I have really enjoyed my time with you today, Patricia. Would you like to meet up again next week?"

"I have enjoyed it, too. So, yes, next week would be good," I replied.

"I will meet you same place, same time then," he said

LOSS OF FAITH

looking pleased, getting up to pay the bill.

I got up and followed him, getting out my purse.

"Oh, no, Patricia, I am paying" he said.

"Oh, thank you," I replied. A proper gentleman.

He walked me back to my car as he wanted to make sure I was safe and we said our good-byes.

He is thoughtful, but maybe he is another Bill? Don't be silly.

We continued to meet up for lunch over the next three months when I was in Sheffield, which was about once every two to three weeks, and we would chat by phone in between.

It was a nice friendship without being serious. So, for me, it was just what the doctor ordered.

Something that would allow me to get to know someone slowly and develop a friendship was all I could deal with right now.

I felt that I was healing from my past and now had a way forward. I was having a good time and very rarely thought of my past. I had a friend to go out with, my job and my singing.

But, I still could not bring myself to renew my faith in God. My memories of having trust and faith resulted in getting hurt and having bad experiences, so I just kept pushing everything away, as I just did not want to know.

I got feelings and thoughts about things, but would not trust those instincts anymore, even if they proved to be right. I had great doubts about what I was being given.

My attitude toward it was: how can I help anyone else if I cannot help myself? If I did not trust what I was given, how could I give it to someone else?

LOSS OF FAITH

This was a very analytical time for me. I was questioning everything. I was very successful in my work but that, in itself, brought its own issues. I did not have many friends because I was always working, and women (and some men) were jealous of what I had achieved.

I could never understand that, because I would be glad if someone had worked hard and achieved what they wanted to achieve. But, being a successful business woman brought about isolation. Men were wary and scared of a successful woman. I just could not seem to win.

I loved developing people, seeing them promoted and helping them move on to better things. That was the biggest satisfaction I got from my work, but it appeared others were not like me.

I was always searching for answers and the deeper meaning of things. I wanted to understand what everything was all about, including the meaning of life.

I found myself reading books in search of my answers. All I learned was this: what will be, will be.

This inward battle left me on a quest to find the truth, and what that was, I was not sure.

Here was this confident person, at work and on stage, but inside, I was falling apart, trying to find the meaning of life and the truth of things.

I could not exactly talk to people at work about it. I would talk to Father, but he would say, "You have to look, read, listen and question, and take from things what you believe, and throw the rest away."

He tried to help by talking things through, but I knew I had to get my own answers. It was good, though, to explore theories and concepts with him.

LOSS OF FAITH

I found this process very confusing, because I thought I would get some definite answers. The more I read, the more it appeared I already knew, and in some instances, I knew more. I did not know why.

Through all of this, my dreams had started again. Some of my answers were coming through my dreams or taking me back into past lives to show me where the information was coming from.

This scared me a bit, as I just was not ready to accept it all. So, I pushed it away and decided to stop searching for answers and get on with my life.

I went back to putting my total energy into work and singing and seeing my daughter, when I could.

Chapter Thirty-Nine

A Simple Kiss

The friendship between Peter and me was growing, slowly, which is what I needed as I was not in a hurry to get tied down. We would go for walks on the weekends during the day. He understood about my work and my singing, so we would do things when we could, and gradually we saw more and more of each other, but purely as friends.

Friendship suited me at this point, but I did wonder if there was something wrong with me or did he just not fancy me in that way? But, at this time, I valued the friendship because my working life and singing, was demanding and now and again I was seeing my daughter.

It's funny. When someone is full on, we think they are after just one thing, and when someone is slow, we wonder what is wrong with us. We can't win either way.

It had been good for me to take time out from relationships, because I had certainly lost myself within each

LOSS OF FAITH

one and did not know who I really was.

Now, I had found myself again, and I loved who I was, and I felt alive again.

I would recommend taking some time out from relationships to find yourself again because you will be amazed at what comes.

Most of us just roll from one relationship to another because we are afraid of being on our own. It is fear itself that stops us from changing patterns that have appeared in our lives, or changing our lives altogether. I know that happened to me.

Once I took the first step, it really was an amazing experience for me. Not only did I find myself again, but it opened up opportunities for me, like my work, singing, a friendship, and even seeing my daughter.

Peter and I always seemed to end up going to the same business functions and, during the weekday evenings, we went out. We would have long debates about what was happening in the world and how to put it right. Things just seemed comfortable between us.

I did notice that when someone asked me to dance, he seemed to be jealous, but he did not say anything because we were just friends. I did wonder what was in his heart and mind, as his behaviour did appear to change in certain circumstances. But, I thought maybe I was reading more into things than I should. I certainly did not want to lose his friendship.

I had known Peter for about six months when we went walking in Derbyshire one Sunday afternoon. We were walking down a hill when I slipped and lost my footing. He quickly grabbed hold of me to stop me totally from falling. He pulled me up and held my hands asking me, "Are you all right?"

"Yes, thanks," I replied.

He kept hold of my hands and looked at me, and then he kissed me. That took me by surprise, but it felt good and right. We started walking again, and he kept hold of one hand. Neither of us said a word but kept walking.

I hope this does not spoil our friendship. I wonder what he is thinking. Here I was again taking a step into a relationship. Could this one be different?

I had my work and my singing, and for the first time I had been focusing on myself and what I wanted to do.

This makes me nervous. Was Peter going to be different and allow me to be me?

I tried to push these thoughts out of my mind.

You are stupid. He has only just kissed you and already your mind is working overtime.

So, I tried just to enjoy the moment without any judgment.

When we got back to the car, Peter asked, "Are you all right, Patricia, with what has happened?"

"Yes," I replied.

On the way home, we talked and everything was relaxed. When we stopped outside my parents' home Peter asked, "I would like for us to go on holiday together, would you like that?"

"Yes, that would be nice," I replied.

"I will organize something. Where would you like to go?" he asked.

"Northumberland," I replied.

"Okay, I will sort it out. I will phone you tomorrow,"

LOSS OF FAITH

he said, as he leaned over and kissed me again.

I got out of the car and went into the house. My heart was racing with excitement.

"You look happy," Father said.

"Yes, I had a good time," I replied.

"That's good," he said.

"I am off to bed now. See you in the morning," I said, as I headed for my bedroom.

My mind would not stop working.

Why Northumberland?

Northumberland was where I lived with Bill. I had left there in such a hurry with bad memories and low self esteem. Maybe there were things I needed to face for myself. I did not want to use Peter in any way and hurt him, but Northumberland had just come tripping out of my mouth without any thought, so it must have been guided.

It made me nervous but I had never really faced that part of my past and maybe, I was not meant to do it on my own.

Chapter Forty

A New Beginning

Father once told me not to talk about my past to anyone because then, if I was starting a new life, with a clean sheet, nobody could use it against me, as they had done before.

Peter was the first person I had not said anything to. We talked about work and the world but we never spoke about our pasts.

He was true to his word and arranged for a week long holiday in September which was two months away. This way, we could both organize our time off.

Our relationship developed and we started seeing each other every night during the week and he would come and hear me sing on the weekends.

When it was time for the holiday, I was very nervous about going, but I knew I had to do it.

We drove there, and as we got closer, I could feel nervousness in my stomach.

LOSS OF FAITH

This is stupid.

We arrived at the cottage, unloaded the car and then, went out to eat. It felt really strange being back in Northumberland. I could remember the roads and everything.

Peter would get his map out to find places and I would just keep quite as I certainly did not want any questions asked. Travelling round did help me face my demons, and I was with a person who I enjoyed being with.

We had a good time and the week went so quickly that we found ourselves packing up to go home.

As we were packing, Peter said, "I have really enjoyed myself this week and I always like being with you. I would like for us to try living together. What do you think?"

"I feel the same. So yes, I would like to try living with you and see what happens," I replied.

I am still afraid of relationships, but I can't let that stop my moving forward. Peter has never been married. What will he be like?

Peter was not a romantic person but it was a big step for him, because he had never lived with anyone before.

We drove home and he dropped me off at my parents' saying, "I will look for a house to rent that is within travelling distance to work for both of us, and then you can look at it to see if you like it,"

"Okay. Thanks for a lovely holiday," I said.

It took about a week for Peter to find a house. It was a terraced house at Mexborough. So, I went to have a look on the weekend in daylight. He picked me up from my parents' and we went straight to the house. It was in a good area and had two bedrooms, bathroom, kitchen and lounge. It didn't have much of a garden, just a shared

LOSS OF FAITH

courtyard at the back. But we both worked, so it was a good option.

"So, what do you think, Patricia," Peter asked.

"I think it is lovely and quaint, perfect," I replied.

"I will sort it out, put the deposit down and it will be in both our names," he said, sounding excited.

He liked organizing things and that was fine by me. It took the pressure off me.

Peter didn't waste much time. Within a week we had signed the paperwork and got the keys to move in.

Over the next few weeks we looked at furniture as the house was unfurnished and bought what we needed to set up home. Peter would not let me pay for anything.

The carpets got fitted and the furniture delivered. It was beginning to look like a home. It was exciting. I was sneaking some of my things out of my parents; house a bit at a time. I knew I had to tell them sometime, but I just did not want my mother to go on and on.

It had been an interesting time, that had ended in my committing myself to living with him.

It was time to tell my parents and surprisingly enough, they seemed to know. Father said, "As long as you know what you are doing and it makes you happy."

"I know, Father, but if I don't try, I will never know. This has gone slowly and I have not rushed. I can only see where it takes me," I replied.

Things started to speed up. Everything had been done by the Wednesday. So, we decided to move in on that Saturday.

I spent the next few days packing my things up and getting them over to the house, so that Saturday morning,

LOSS OF FAITH

I just had a few things to take.

I had pushed God and everything away and was making this decision on my own. I just could not find things within myself to have trust and faith anymore.

On Friday night, I had a dream so clear and vivid. I saw myself moving into the house and six months later getting married. I woke up.

No way am I getting married. Just go away and leave me alone. I don't want any more to do with you. I don't want your dreams or anything else. I want a normal life.

Saturday morning came and it did seem strange. I had my breakfast and loaded my car. It was difficult to leave my parents' house, as it had been a source of safety for me, and now, that safety net was being pulled away. I cried as I kissed my mother and father goodbye. As I drove away, I looked back to see them and tears were streaming down my face.

Was I doing the right thing?

Photos

Patricia aged 26

LOSS OF FAITH

My daughter Angela aged 7

My daughter Angela aged 9

LOSS OF FAITH

My sister, Angela, and me at
my wedding to Steve.

Patricia, aged 28,
with a friend at her wedding to Bill

LOSS OF FAITH

My daughter, Angela, aged 7 with me.

My wedding to Steve age 25.

LOSS OF FAITH

My daughter, Angela, aged 9 with me.

My sister, Angela, and me with my
daughter, Angela, aged 9.

LOSS OF FAITH

My daughter Angela age 11
on holiday in Morpeth with me and Bill.

My daughter Angela aged 7 and my brother
Terry's children, Emma and Terry.

LOSS OF FAITH

Family picture, Mother, Father, Brother Terry and his wife Nora, Daughter Angela aged 7 and my brother's children Emma and Terry.

Patricia's sports car
in Crasters Northumberland aged 28

LOSS OF FAITH

Patricia's wedding to Steve age 25.

Patricia aged 28 in Crasters Northumberland.

Also by Patricia Milner

She could remember every detail. Every line, flaw and feature was burned into her memory forever. Whether it was the intricate design of the crochet blanket in the back of the rapist's truck, or the smile on her dead grandfather's face when he spoke to her at his own funeral, her vivid memory was just a small side effect of her increasing psychic skills. Growing up with a foot in several dimensions was not easy.

Patricia Milner's poetry is inspired by reflecting on her life. When she began writing poetry, she was seeing clients that reminded her of where she used to be. She would be working on her computer and forget what she was doing. She found herself typing and when she had finished she had written a poem. Then she would remember what she was originally doing. A few days later, she would see a client and have the urge to read the poem to them. The client would say "That's how I feel about my life and what I want to happen." The poems kept on coming and the same thing with clients kept occurring. This inspired her to share the poems and create her book of poems. She hopes all her readers will get the inspiration that she has seen happen with her clients. The channelled poems have already had an impact on many people's lives. Hopefully, they will help you too.

ABOUT THE AUTHOR

Patricia Milner is an International Psychic Medium, Reiki Master, Spiritual Trainer, Teacher and Author. She comes from a family of psychic mediums and healers and has been able to connect with spirits from a very early age. Professional she worked as a Human Resources Director and later ran her own Human Resources business. For many years Patricia has been sharing her natural psychic medium gift with people, helping clients cope with difficult times, create a new path for themselves and providing guidance as they progress along their spiritual path. Patricia has also used her medium and psychic abilities to give closure to many people whose loved ones have crossed over into the spirit world. Her ability allows her to channel information directly from the spirit level. Over the years her healing work has developed into Emotional Freedom Therapy having many successes. Patricia has written articles for national magazines and is an expert author on Ezine.com. She also appears in national magazines, on numerous radio and TV interview programs.

Visit Patricia's website at: www.yourspiritualworld.com

All Patricia's books are available on Amazon.com, BN.com. Divine Intervention and Loss of Faith are eBooks for the iPad, the Kindle, the Nook, the Kobo and more.

www.ingramcontent.com/pod-product-compliance
Lightning Source LLC
Chambersburg PA
CBHW052014070526
44584CB00016B/1746